Delish!

A MARTHA'S VINEYARD COOKBOOK

Delish!

THE J. W. JACKSON RECIPES

BY PHILIP R. CRAIG AND SHIRLEY PRADA CRAIG

Published by Vineyard Stories
RR1 Box 65B9
Edgartown, MA 02539
508-221-2338
info@vineyardstories.com

The publishers wish to acknowledge support on this project provided by
Bookhouse Group, Inc. (www.bookhouse.net) in Atlanta, GA.

Library of Congress Control Number: 2006929256

ISBN: 0-9771384-2-9

Manufactured in Canada

Book design by Jill Dible
Cover Photo: Betsy Corsiglia
Illustrations: Jack Sherman
Editor: John Walter

This book is dedicated to all of the wonderful cooks who have shared their recipes and made our taste buds dance with joy.

— Shirley and Philip Craig

TABLE OF CONTENTS

PREFACE

"Be wary of any recipe over four inches long."

—J. W. Jackson

My wife, Shirley Prada Craig, was born on Martha's Vineyard, as were her father and his father, and as were our children and two of our five grandchildren. I'm the only off-islander in the family. I would like to have been island-born, but had no voice in the matter and was, instead, born in California, and raised, from age three, on a small cattle ranch ten miles southeast of Durango, Colorado. It's pretty far from saltwater.

Shirley's parents both had Azorean ancestors. Her father was an excellent fisherman and her mother was an excellent cook, so Shirley grew up eating and cooking fresh fish and shellfish, traditional Portuguese foods such as Masa Sovada, and kale soup.

Nana's Steamed Pudding, a favorite holiday dessert, was made by her paternal grandmother, who was Scottish, and who, when Shirley was of age, handed her the steamer mold with the pronouncement, "It's your turn now, dear." Shirley has made this family favorite every Christmas since.

Out in Colorado, my parents fed five children food grown on their ranch: beef, chicken, rabbit, eggs, bread made from flour milled from their own wheat, vegetables grown in their garden, and the meat of deer and elk my father killed every fall. My mother cooked everything on a woodstove, and for many years, in the winter, the morning and evening meals were eaten by lamplight because there was no electricity in the house. My early cooking was mostly done in a frying pan on that kitchen stove and over campfires in mountain cattle camps.

While Shirley was growing up, she went to the mainland once every other year, on a shopping trip to New Bedford with her grandmother. Until she attended Sargent College, then in Cambridge, to study physical therapy, she had never been to Boston, and when she got there she learned that most of her classmates had never even heard of Martha's Vineyard. (Times have changed.)

Meanwhile, I had gone to Boston University for several reasons: I had never been further east than Kansas; I could live with an uncle and thus save a lot of housing money I didn't have; I could study religion and philosophy (a major consistent with my intention of becoming a minister—a notion later abandoned, much to the relief of the Baptist Church); and, most importantly, BU had a fencing team and I, as a result of having seen too many Errol Flynn movies, was set upon becoming the best fencer in the world.

As fate would have it, back on the Vineyard Shirley's high school French teacher had interested her, too, in fencing; and in 1953, at Salle Elde, a private fencing club in Cambridge, we literally met over crossed swords when her regular instructor was absent one evening and the maitre d'arms of the club asked me to take over her class.

Right away, I found myself *interested* in this person. But even if I'd had the nerve to ask Shirley over to my apartment for a home-cooked meal—which I didn't—I wouldn't have been much of a host. In those days I cooked bacon and eggs for breakfast, winter squash and hamburger purchased at Boston's open market for lunch and dinner, and very little else. Eventually I did invite her over, and she cooked. And did the dishes. And we continued to see each other at fencing.

In the spring of 1955, at the end of the semester, I went, on a whim, to Martha's Vineyard. The whim had a name: Shirley. I had never been on an island, and I had imagined it to be a mound of sand with a palm tree in the middle. I was astonished to discover that the Vineyard had electricity, and I fell instantly in love with its beauty.

I asked for and received directions to Shirley's house, and went there, but Shirley was leaving that very day for a mainland visit to friends. Knowing that she'd be back, I got a job on a scow, and worked that summer rebuilding docks that had been destroyed by devastating hurricanes the year before. When she returned, Shirley, her parents, and her grandmother fed me vast amounts of food, all of which I devoured while gaining not a pound. (Times have changed.)

In 1957, Shirley and I graduated from Boston University and went to Colorado. There we were married. In the following months, we ate a lot of forgettable meals, the worst of which was an experiment with canned okra that fifty years later is still vividly remembered as "green slime."

In 1958, and off and on for the next four years, we were in Iowa City, Iowa, attending the Iowa Writers Workshop and eating starving student food: casseroles made of canned tuna and crushed potato chips, macaroni and cheese and canned salmon, Dinty Moore Beef Stew Curry, and other such meals. We had no car and thus could not take advantage of the succulent fifteen-cent burgers at McDonald's on the far side of town.

On the Vineyard, where we worked when we weren't in school, we became owners of an old hunting camp and a sixty-five-dollar car, which we drove to Iowa and back. Shirley and other student wives exchanged recipes and became experts at making good meals on minimum budgets, and I began trying to write novels. As this was going on, our family expanded to four.

Upon graduation, I began teaching at Endicott Junior College in Beverly, Massachusetts. Our family summered on the Vineyard and wintered in Hamilton while I wrote books that didn't sell. About that time, I had a sudden nostalgia for the homemade white bread my mother had baked long ago on the ranch woodstove. I baked four loaves, using the recipe in the old red Betty Crocker cookbook—and they were delish!

That was the real beginning of my interest in cooking, which took its highest form later, when a small group of men friends and I would prepare elegant, multicoursed, gourmet meals for our wives.

All of this time, of course, Shirley was doing most of the cooking and getting better by the day, though always with a small budget, and with children to feed. She remains, to this day, the principal and best cook in the house.

In 1965, I started teaching at Wheelock College, and in 1969 finally had my first novel, *Gate of Ivory, Gate of Horn*, published. Delighted to be able to think of myself as a "writer," I wrote another book. It did not sell. I wrote another. It didn't sell, either. I began to identify myself as an "ex-writer," but kept on writing and cooking for the next twenty years until finally, in 1989, *A Beautiful Place to Die* was published. Therein, J. W. Jackson and Zee Madieras Jackson made their first appearance. That was nineteen novels ago. Number twenty will appear in the spring of 2007.

From the beginning of the Jackson-Madieras romance, food was an important element in their lives, and it has continued to be through the subsequent novels in the series. This book is a response to many requests from readers over the years for a J.W. cookbook.

––––––

The island of Martha's Vineyard lies off the southern coast of Cape Cod. It is an emerald rimmed by a circle of gold set in a sapphire sea. A few thousand people live there during the winter, and eight or ten times that number live there during the summer. The islanders are glad to see the tourist money come and, in the fall, glad to see the visitors go.

The waters surrounding the Vineyard are full of fish and lobsters, and its ponds are home to scallops, clams, crabs, oysters, and mussels. The island is dotted with farms and gardens where good things are grown and sold in local markets. Wild edible foods—including lambs quarter, grapes, sassafras, and mushrooms—are abundant, and for hunters the forests are full of deer, and the ponds are home to geese and ducks.

As we do, the Jacksons live in a house overlooking Sengekontacket Pond, and, as we do, they enjoy cooking and eating all the island's foods and more besides. Like us, they surf-cast for bluefish, bonito, Spanish Mackerel, and bass; go shellfishing; and have vegetable gardens from which they harvest whatever is in season. Like us, they preserve what they can't eat fresh, sometimes barter for venison and game birds, bake their own bread, and keep vodka in the freezer. They, too, enjoy Greek, Spanish, Thai, Portuguese, and other foreign foods, as well as the meals they typically cook from island produce.

This book contains some of our—and their—favorite recipes. The emphasis on fish dishes, breads, and homegrown vegetables is a reflection on our lives as islanders; we live in a place where many meals are eaten outdoors and where winter entertainment often consists of sharing food with friends beside a warming fire. A number of the recipes are actually over four inches long, but they're worth cooking anyhow. If some of them look familiar, it's because the Jacksons and the Craigs believe that once they've cooked something, the recipe is theirs. We borrow, steal, and alter recipes without shame, and we advise you to do the same.

Philip R. Craig

Edgartown, Massachusetts
Autumn 2006

A FEW NOTES ON THESE RECIPES

"If you can read, you can cook."

—J. W. Jackson

- Unless otherwise specified, extra-virgin olive oil is the cooking and salad oil of choice.

- Unsalted butter is preferred over the salted kind, and flour is the all-purpose variety.

- When a recipe calls for mayonnaise, cream cheese, sour cream, or Ricotta cheese, you may use the reduced-fat equivalents unless the directions specify the full-fat variety.

- Fresh ingredients are almost always preferred to the dried, canned, or frozen kind, when they are available and of good quality.

- Freshly grated pepper and nutmeg are superior to the already-processed forms.

- If you must substitute dried herbs for fresh ones, use $1/3$ less.

- Under-salt rather than over-salt. Eaters can always add more salt at the table if they want it.

- Serving sizes in this book may vary depending on the number and appetites of the eaters. Portions, as listed, tend to be on the generous side.

- Feel free to alter these recipes according to your tastes.

If you have any recommendations for changes and are willing to share your thoughts, write to J.W. and Zee at sjcraig@adelphia.net or prcraig@adelphia.net. Thanks in advance.

Delish!

Breakfasts and Brunches

"I WENT BACK INTO THE KITCHEN
AND GOT MYSELF SOME PANCAKES;
THE COOK IS OFTEN THE LAST
TO EAT. THEY WERE WORTH
WAITING FOR."

—J.W., IN *VINEYARD SHADOWS*

WEAKFISH BREAKFAST

Weakfish are hard to find these days, but if one jumps onto your line, bring it home and have it for breakfast.

—Zee

Fry sliced potatoes in butter until tender; keep warm.

Fry filleted weakfish (lightly dredged with seasoned flour) in butter (add more to pan if necessary).

Serve with poached eggs and toasted homemade bread.

SMOKED BLUEFISH ON BAGELS WITH CREAM CHEESE AND ONION

The Craigs and the Jacksons often eat this dish for breakfast or for snacks. Delish!

—J.W.

Lightly toast the best bagel you can find.

Spread it with cream cheese and top with chunks of smoked bluefish and very thinly sliced red onion.

CRAB TOASTS WITH ASPARAGUS

3 tbsp. good mayonnaise at room temperature

1–2 tsp. whole-grain Dijon mustard (or to taste)

1–2 tsp. fresh lemon juice (to taste)

$^1/_2$ lb. crabmeat, cleaned of shell bits, at room temperature

16 asparagus spears of medium thickness, trimmed to 4″ length (reserve bottom ends for another purpose)

$^1/_2$ tbsp. butter, melted

4 thin slices white bread, crusts trimmed

4 very thin slices lemon

Jeff and I enjoy this in the spring and early summer when the asparagus bed offers up new, tasty stalks on a daily basis. Green gold!

—Zee

Mix mayonnaise, mustard, and 1 tsp. lemon juice together. Taste for flavor before adding second tsp. lemon juice. Stir enough of this mixture into crabmeat to bind it.

Cook asparagus to crisp tender. Drain spears and roll in melted butter.

Toast bread lightly on both sides. Spread crabmeat on toasts and place on warmed serving dishes. Arrange 4 asparagus spears on top of each (or in rectangle around toast slices) and garnish with lemon slices.

Serve at once.

Serves 2 as a main course or 4 as a side dish. It makes an excellent brunch dish.

Note: This recipe can be morphed into the following form, which may be superior: Substitute warmed croissants (sliced lengthwise) for the toast, smoked salmon or bluefish for the crabmeat, hollandaise sauce for the sauce, and caviar for the garnish.

LOBSTER, CROISSANTS, AND CHAMPAGNE

1 (1¹/₂-lb.) lobster per person
As many croissants as the breakfasters can eat
As much champagne as people want to drink

The name says it all.
J.W. and Zee have this
sinful meal once or twice
a year, usually for
brunch, and it's always
a success. This recipe
first appeared in the
back of Dead in
Vineyard Sand.

—Shirley

Steam the lobsters. When done, use shears to cut open the bodies, legs, and claws; drain off excess water; and serve the lobsters with croissants, champagne, and lots of melted butter, napkins, and paper towels. Lobster bibs are recommended if you're eating in anything but your bathing suit—or in nothing at all.

*"He received us in his
quietly genial fashion . . .
and joined us in a hearty meal."*
—A. CONAN DOYLE, THE ENGINEER'S THUMB

ASPARAGUS PIE

Filling:

1 cup shredded, mild Cheddar cheese (preferably white)

$^1/_2$ cup good mayonnaise

1 tsp. lemon juice

1$^1/_2$ cups asparagus (cooked to crisp tender and cut into bite-sized pieces)

Slivered almonds

Crust:

(Note: You may use refrigerated biscuit dough to line the pie pan instead of making your own crust.)

1 cup flour

2 tsp. baking powder

$^1/_4$ tsp. salt

$^1/_4$ cup vegetable shortening (like Crisco)

$^1/_2$ cup cold milk

Dijon mustard

Mix dry ingredients together. Cut in shortening until mixture consists of small crumblike particles. Stir in milk and mix lightly (do not overmix).

Roll out dough to fit 9″ pie pan. Spread crust with a small amount of prepared mustard.

Mix filling ingredients together and pour into biscuit dough crust. Bake in preheated 350° oven for about $^1/_2$ hour. Pie may be covered well and frozen before baking. Thaw completely before baking.

Makes 6 servings

This recipe was given by Shirley to J.W., who now claims it as his own. It is a nice offering for a brunch buffet; sun-dried tomato rings or red pepper strips make a colorful garnish. We first included the recipe in Dead in Vineyard Sand.

—Phil

SPINACH QUICHE

1 small onion
1/2 lb. sliced mushrooms
1–2 tbsp. butter
1 cup shredded Swiss cheese (almost 8 oz.)
1/4 cup freshly grated Parmesan cheese
1 cup cream
1/2 cup milk
3 eggs
1/2 tsp. nutmeg
Salt and pepper to taste
Dash cayenne pepper
1 pkg. (10-oz.) frozen, chopped spinach, thawed and well drained to remove as much water as possible
2–3 strips bacon, cooked crisp and crumbled (optional)
1 (9") pie shell, unbaked

Even real men like J.W. and Phil enjoy this classic.

—Shirley

Sauté onions and mushrooms in butter. Beat cream, milk, and eggs together. Add spices, cheeses, onions, mushrooms, spinach, and bacon bits to egg mixture. Smear crust with soft butter before pouring filling into crust.

Bake in preheated 350° oven for 40–50 minutes or until knife inserted in center comes out clean. Serve warm.

Quiche may be decorated with pimiento or roasted red pepper slices before serving.

Once baked, quiche may be cooled, wrapped well, and frozen. Thaw before reheating.

Makes 6–8 wedges

ZUCCHINI OMELET

4 eggs
1/4 cup milk
1 small zucchini, grated
1 tbsp. grated onion
1/2 cup grated Cheddar cheese
2 tbsp. butter
Salt and pepper to taste
Paprika

Zooklear disarmament! When the neighbors will no longer accept your gifts of surplus zucchini, invite them over for brunch.

—Shirley

Heat unsalted butter in skillet or omelet pan until hot but not smoking. Sauté zucchini and onions.

Beat eggs with whisk until blended, then beat in milk, salt, and pepper. Pour eggs over zucchini and onion. Cook over low heat, lifting edges with a spatula to allow uncooked portions to run to bottom.

When eggs are almost set, sprinkle with grated cheese and fold in half. Sprinkle with paprika and serve immediately with freshly toasted homemade bread.

ENGLISH SCONES

4 cups flour
2 tbsp. sugar
4 tsp. baking powder
1 tsp. salt
½ tsp. cream of tartar
⅔ cup cold butter
1⅓ cups half-and-half
1 large egg
¼ cup chopped apricots, candied orange or lemon peel,
crystallized ginger, or golden raisins (if desired)

J. W. Jackson has never been to England, but Shirley has. She came home loving the British Full Cream Tea that she had in the Pump Room in Bath, and often bakes up a batch of scones for favored houseguests' early-morning arrivals.

—Phil

In large bowl, combine dry ingredients. Cut in butter, with pastry blender or 2 knives, until mixture resembles coarse crumbs.

In small bowl, beat together half-and-half and egg. Reserve 2 tbsp. of mixture. Add remaining mixture to dry ingredients and mix in chopped fruits, if using. Mix lightly with fork only until mixture clings together and forms a soft dough.

Turn mixture out onto lightly floured surface and knead gently about 6 times. Do not use too much flour or knead too long. Divide dough in half. Roll or pat half of dough into a 7" round. Cut round into 4–6 wedges. Repeat with remaining dough.

Place scones, 1" apart, on greased baking sheet. Pierce tops with tines of fork. Brush tops with reserved egg mixture and sprinkle with sugar (or combination of sugar and cinnamon) if desired. Bake in preheated 425° oven for 15–18 minutes or until golden brown.

Serve warm with Devonshire cream (see below), or butter, and jam or lemon curd.

Makes 10–12 scones

DEVONSHIRE-STYLE CREAM

3 oz. light cream cheese
1 tsp. sugar
1 cup heavy cream, at room temperature

Beat together cream cheese and sugar with electric mixer on medium-high speed until mixture is light and fluffy. Add heavy cream and beat on high speed until stiff peaks form. Cover and refrigerate overnight. Serve with warm scones and jam or lemon curd.

Devonshire cream (also known as clotted cream) is served with tea, scones, and jam to constitute the properly famous British Full Cream Tea.

—Shirley

APRICOT-ALMOND OATMEAL SCONES

1 cup quick oats
$^1/_2$ cup slivered almonds
$^1/_4$ cup milk
$^1/_4$ cup heavy cream
1 large egg
$1^1/_2$ cups unbleached flour
$^1/_3$ cup granulated sugar
2 tsp. baking powder
$^1/_2$ tsp. salt
10 tbsp. unsalted butter, cold and cut into $^1/_2$″ cubes
$^1/_2$ cup dried apricots, chopped finely
granulated sugar for sprinkling

Shirley likes these scones even better than the regular ones! Me, too!

—Phil

Adjust oven rack to middle position; heat oven to 375°. Spread oats and almonds evenly on baking sheet and toast in oven until fragrant and lightly browned (7–9 minutes). Cool on wire rack. Increase oven temperature to 450° (we used 425° in our oven). Line second baking sheet with parchment paper. When oats are cooled, measure out 2 tbsp. and set aside.

Whisk milk, cream, and egg in large measuring cup until incorporated; remove 1 tbsp. to small bowl and reserve for glazing.

Pulse flour, $^1/_3$ cup sugar, baking powder, and salt in food processor until combined. Scatter cold butter evenly over dry ingredients and pulse until mixture resembles coarse cornmeal (12–14 1-second pulses). Transfer mixture to bowl; stir in oat mixture and apricots. Fold in liquid ingredients until large clumps form. Mix dough by hand in bowl until dough forms a cohesive mass.

Dust work surface with reserved oats. Turn dough out onto work surface and dust with remaining oats. Gently pat into 7″ circle about 1″ thick. Cut dough into 8 wedges and set on parchment lined baking sheet, leaving 2″ between scones. Brush surfaces with reserved egg mixture and sprinkle with sugar. Bake until golden (12–14 minutes). Cool on baking sheet on wire rack for 5 minutes, then remove scones to cooling rack.

Serve with Devonshire cream and your favorite jam. Enjoy!

Makes 8 scones

"Breakfast is the most important meal of the day. So are the others."
—J. W. JACKSON

BRETON CREPES

1 cup plus 2 tbsp. buckwheat flour
1 tsp. sea salt
1 egg
water

More evidence that French cuisine is the best in the world. When we traveled in Brittany, we discovered Breton Crepes and then spent a lot of time finding a Breton cookbook that would tell us how to make them. It was worth the work.

—Shirley and Phil

Put the flour in a mixing bowl, leaving a small hollow in the center. Put the egg and the salt in the hollow. Mix with a wooden spoon, adding water little by little until the mixture is the consistency of thick mayonnaise. Mix energetically for about 10 minutes. Add more water while mixing to obtain a final consistency of cream. This may take some experimentation but is no more difficult than making regular crepes.

Ladle or pour a small amount of batter into a hot, very lightly greased skillet, and quickly rotate pan so that batter covers the bottom evenly. When the edges start to lift away from the pan, turn carefully with a spatula and cook the other side just until lightly browned.

Crepes should not be crispy. Stir the batter frequently to keep proper consistency.

Breton Crepes can be filled or garnished with a variety of foods, depending on the time of day you are serving them. Jeff and Zee enjoy them simply served with Breton Herb Butter.

Makes about 24 6″ crepes

BRETON HERB BUTTER

Parsley
Chervil
Chives
Watercress
Shallot
Garlic
Pepper to taste

Finely chop any or all of the above and mix with slightly
salted butter. The Breton butter should have a nice green
color. It can be slathered on plain Breton Crepes or used to
enhance other fillings.

Optional Fillings or Garnishes for Breton Crepes
Egg
Smoked fish or sausage
Cheese
Cooked fruits
Fruit preserves
Sardines
Soft cheese
Tomato slices with fresh herbs

BLINI WITH CAVIAR

2¹/₂ cups milk
¹/₄ cup unsalted butter
3 cups flour (buckwheat is best) sifted with 3 tbsp. sugar
and 1 tsp. salt
3 egg yolks
1 pkg. dry yeast, mixed with ¹/₄ cup warm water
3 egg whites

Toppings:
¹/₂ cup melted butter
3¹/₂–4 oz. salmon or black lumpfish caviar
1 pint sour cream

Phil and I discovered these in the now-defunct Russian Tea Room in New York City. After some experimentation, we deem this recipe a successful re-creation of those tasty Russian offerings. They're good with Bloody Marys.

—Shirley

Three hours in advance of serving, bring milk and butter to just below boiling. Cool. Beat egg yolks until foamy. Alternately stir flour mixture and milk mixture into egg yolks. Stir in yeast-water mixture. Cover and let rise in a warm place for 1 hour.

Beat egg whites until stiff but not dry. Fold into batter. Let rise again to previous height.

Drop a scant ¹/₄ cup batter, for each blini, on preheated, very lightly greased griddle. Lightly brown on both sides. Keep warm until serving. Serve toppings with blini for guests to choose from.

Makes about 36 blinis

BANANA SMOOTHIE

2 cups frozen raspberries or strawberries
1 banana, sliced
1 cup vanilla yogurt

Whirl all ingredients together in blender until smooth.

If using fresh berries, add ¼ cup crushed ice to blender.

Does it get any healthier? Potassium to go. Our granddaughter, Jessica Harmon, often whips up interesting concoctions in the blender. This is one of them.

—Phil and Shirley

JESSICA'S FRUIT SMOOTHIE

1 nectarine, peeled and cut into chunks
1 banana, sliced
⅛ cup raspberry sherbet
2½ cups cranberry-apple cocktail juice (or any other cranberry/fruit combination)

Here's another good one!
—Phil and Shirley

Whirl all ingredients together in blender until smooth.

PLOUGHMAN'S LUNCH

*When we travel in
Britain, we often eat
in pubs, where we can
get pints of the best
bitter and simple, fairly
inexpensive food.
Nothing is simpler than
a Ploughman's Lunch.*

—Phil

The typical Ploughman's Lunch consists of:

A slab of crusty bread
A hunk of good Cheddar-type cheese
and
Some Ploughman's Pickle (or Branston Pickle; available in
ethnic grocery stores)

A small side salad is sometimes served with this popular
British pub dish.

NOVA LOX AND EGGS WITH ASPARAGUS

*This is an elegant
breakfast reminiscent of
Eggs Benedict but even
better. Try surprising
your significant other
on a special occasion
with this offering.*

—Shirley

4 large croissants, split lengthwise and lightly toasted
12–16 oz. Nova smoked salmon, sliced. Buy the best you
can afford.
24 spears asparagus, cooked to crisp tender. Use more if
asparagus stalks are very thin.
8 large eggs, poached
hollandaise sauce (see page 168)

Place toasted croissants on heated plates. Top each half with
slices of Nova smoked salmon. Lay 3 asparagus spears on
each croissant half, and top with a poached egg. Spoon hollandaise sauce over eggs, sprinkle with a little paprika, and
scatter a few capers over all.

Pass the Bloody Marys.

Serves 4

Hors d'Oeuvres

"I NEVER GET TIRED OF SMOKED BLUEFISH,
SO I FREEZE IT FOR THAT PURPOSE. DOWN
MY DRIVEWAY I'M FAMOUS FOR MY SMOKED
BLUEFISH ... IF YOU DON'T LIKE IT, WE CAN
STILL BE FRIENDS, BUT OUR RELATIONSHIP
WILL BE UNDER CONSIDERABLE STRAIN."

— J.W., IN *A BEAUTIFUL PLACE TO DIE*

LITTLENECKS ON THE HALF SHELL

The raw-seafood rule is that 50 percent of the people love it, and 50 percent won't eat it. J.W. and Zee are in the eating percent, and prepare this dish in many books.

—Phil

For this popular Vineyard appetizer, use very fresh cherry-stone (1¹/₂–2″ size) quahogs. These are easier to open after they've rested a while in the refrigerator (do not jostle them) or have been nuked about 6 at a time in the microwave oven for about 10 seconds. Spread opened half-shells, with their succulent morsels loosened from the shell, on a cold tray and serve with cocktail sauce or lemon. People who like them will eat a lot, so be prepared.

SCALLOPS WRAPPED IN BACON

October 1 is the birthdate of our first child and opening day of Edgartown's scalloping season for those holding family permits. What better birthday gift than a bushel of fresh bay scallops, some of which can be made into this delicious hors d'oeuvre?

—Shirley

(Amounts depend upon number being served as an appetizer.)
Fresh bay scallops
Bacon strips

Dry scallops on paper toweling. Wrap each scallop in a bacon strip cut to fit and secure with a wooden toothpick.

Broil until bacon is crisp.

STUFFED QUAHOGS

24 large quahogs (hard-shelled New England clams)
1/4 lb. ground kielbasa or linguica
1/4 cup minced onion
1/4 cup chopped celery
1/4 cup chopped green pepper
2 cups fresh bread crumbs, or half bread crumbs and half
Ritz cracker crumbs
1/2 tsp. Herbes de Provence
1 clove garlic, minced
Bacon (24 small squares)
1/2 cup melted butter
A little black pepper
Dash hot pepper sauce (optional)

J.W. prepares stuffers in several books. A variation of the recipe is found at the back of Vineyard Blues. *I think this one is even better.*

—Phil

Saute onion, celery, and green pepper in a little butter, until soft.

Steam quahogs just until they open. Reserve liquid; coarsely chop quahog meat in food processor or meat grinder. Mix all ingredients together, moistening with some of the reserved liquid if necessary. Spray cleaned half-shells with cooking spray. Mound filling loosely in each shell, drizzle with melted butter, and top with a square of uncooked bacon. Bake on cookie sheet in 400° oven until bacon is crisp and stuffing is heated through. Garnish with a sprig of parsley.

Serves 6–8 as an appetizer

CLAMS CASINO

6–8 medium sized (2–3″ diameter) quahogs (hard-shelled New England clams) per person

Sauce for 12–16 quahogs
¼ lb. melted butter
3 crushed garlic cloves
1 tsp. lemon juice
1 tbsp. finely chopped parsley
2 tbsp. chopped chives
Bacon, cut in squares
Dash of hot sauce (optional)

People who won't eat littlenecks on the half-shell gobble these up as fast as they can. There are a lot of recipes for clams casino. This is our favorite. J.W. prepares this in several books; our recipe was first printed in A Deadly Vineyard Holiday.

—Zee

Mix sauce ingredients together and let stand in a warm place for several hours for the flavors to amalgamate.

To each clam on the half-shell (drained of liquid), add 1 teaspoon of butter sauce. Cover with a small square of bacon and broil, about 5″ from heat source, until bacon is crisp.

"It is the part of a wise man to feed himself with moderate pleasant food and drink."
—SPINOZA

BLUEFISH SEVICHE

2 cups of ¹/₂-inch cubes of bluefish fillets
2 small hot green peppers, finely chopped (jalapenos are good)
1 large tomato, peeled and chopped
¹/₂ cup coarsely chopped onion
¹/₄ cup finely chopped sweet red peppers
1¹/₂ cloves garlic, minced
¹/₂ cup tomato juice
¹/₃ cup fresh lime juice
¹/₃ cup olive oil
1 tbsp. parsley, finely chopped
¹/₂ tsp. cilantro, finely chopped
2 thyme sprigs, finely chopped
Salt and pepper to taste

Combine all ingredients and let stand in refrigerator overnight. (Bonito may be used in place of bluefish.) Be sure fish is ocean fresh as the only "cooking" is done by the lime juice.

Serve ice cold.

This has to be one of the best uses for that first run of bluefish in May. Really fresh fish is imperative, and even though the list of ingredients looks a bit long, your first bluefish of the season deserves this special treatment, and you deserve this delectable offering as part of your celebration of the return of the blues.

J.W. makes this in Cliff Hanger, *reissued as* Vineyard Fear, *and the recipe appeared at the back of* Murder at a Vineyard Mansion.

—Phil

SMOKED BLUEFISH

Brine:
1/2 cup kosher salt
1/2 cup granulated sugar (may use partly brown sugar)
1 quart water
Squeeze of fresh lemon juice

This is the best way to use those fillets we freeze after a bluefish blitz. We caught, brined, smoked, and sold many hundreds of pounds of smoked bluefish when we were active in the West Tisbury Farmers' Market, and we rarely came home with anything left in our old "touring car" insulated box..

—Shirley

Mix enough of the above brine ingredients in the proportions given to cover the number of bluefish fillets you have. Put fillets in a nonreactive pan or dish and leave them, refrigerated, for at least 12 hours. Thoroughly rinse brine from fillets, towel dry, and place fillets on wire racks to air dry until dry to the touch (time required depends upon temperature and humidity). Be sure to protect fish as it is drying from flying or crawling insects and resident cats.

Place fish on racks in smoker with a pan of dampened hickory (or other flavored wood) chips in pan above heat source. Smoke over low heat, replacing wood chips as needed, until fillets are golden and meat is opaque. Time will vary depending on size of smoker, heat source and temperature, and number of fillets, etc. Usually a few hours of smoking are required.

Remove fish from smoker and cool on racks before wrapping in plastic wrap (and again in aluminum foil if you're going to freeze them).

Wrapped fish may be frozen but should be thawed between layers of paper towels to remove excess moisture before serving.

Note: Previously frozen raw fillets may be thawed and used in the above recipe with very good results.

Smoked bluefish goes well with the following sauce.

MUSTARD, DILL, AND CAPER SAUCE

3 tbsp. Dijon-type mustard
2 tbsp. sugar
2–3 tsp. fresh lemon juice
¾ tsp. dry mustard
3 tbsp. vegetable oil
3 tbsp. drained capers
3 tbsp. fresh dill, chopped
Freshly ground black pepper
Party-size pumpernickel or rye bread slices

Whisk first 4 ingredients together in a bowl. Gradually whisk in oil, then stir in remaining ingredients. Cover and chill until serving time. Serve with smoked fish and bread slices. This recipe makes enough for about 1 lb. of smoked fish.

You might also try this sauce spooned over mussels served on the half-shell or with any number of fish dishes.

Presentation may not be everything, but it helps. Line an oval platter (fish-shaped would be great) with Bibb lettuce leaves. Place a whole fillet of smoked fish on top. Garnish with lemon slices and sprigs of fresh dill and serve accompanied by this sauce. The sauce may be made up to three days ahead of serving and kept, covered, in the refrigerator.

—Shirley

SMOKED BLUEFISH PATE

*The pièce de résistance!
Take a tub of this
concoction to a cocktail
or dinner party, and
you're bound to be
invited again. It's J.W.'s
most popular hors
d'oeuvre, and he and
Zee eat it in many of
Phil's books. The recipe
was published in* A
Shoot on Martha's
Vineyard.

—Shirley

5–6 oz. shredded smoked bluefish
8 oz. whipped cream cheese*
¹/₂ tbsp. finely diced red onion*
1 tsp. prepared horseradish
1 tsp. lemon juice
Dash of Worcestershire sauce if desired
*Or omit onion and use whipped cream cheese with chives

Mix all ingredients together by hand. Serve on plain crackers, pita wedges, or bagel chips.

SOYBEAN APPETIZER

*J.W. wishes this fine
appetizer had a more
appealing name, but it
doesn't. Try it anyway.
You'll like it.*

—Zee

Steam whole soybeans (in pod) over boiling water for 6–8 minutes. Drain and run under cold water. Pat dry and chill.

Serve, sprinkled with coarse salt. Eat by stripping beans from pod with your teeth (much like stripping the tender parts from artichoke leaves).

Yummy as a healthy snack or hors d'oeuvre.

CALAMARI (Fried Squid Rings)

6 small to medium squid
2 eggs, beaten
1 cup vegetable or peanut oil
½ cup flour
Salt to taste (add a small amount of cayenne pepper if you like them spicy)

Clean fresh squid and dry thoroughly. Some prefer to remove the tentacles, but if they are not too large, they can be quite tender and very good. Cut body into rings. Dip the rings (and tentacles, if using) into the beaten egg, then into seasoned flour. Shake off excess flour and fry in hot (350°) oil until evenly brown (no more than 3–5 minutes). Do not overcook, or squid will toughen.

Serve immediately with lemon wedges and seasoned mayonnaise or tartar sauce.

Serves 6

Okay, squid is just bait for most fishermen, but they're more than that to Phil and me. We and our two children, Kim and Jamie, first discovered fried calamari when we lived in a little coastal town in Spain in 1973. Our daughter cried for most of a week after our departure because she could no longer frequent Maricel's Café for calamari and lemonade. All these years later, we try to pacify her with our version when she visits.

—Shirley

TONI'S SPICY SHRIMP

1³/₄ lbs. raw shrimp
1 tbsp. unsalted butter
1 tbsp. olive oil
1 tbsp. minced garlic
2 tbsp. shallots, minced
Salt and pepper to taste
2 tbsp. lemon juice
2 tbsp. fresh dill, chopped

Toni Chute, indulging my gluttonous appetite for shrimp, first served this dish to Phil and me at her Konomika Point home. I, of course, immediately stole the recipe.

—Shirley

Peel and devein shrimp.
Melt butter with olive oil in skillet. Add garlic and shallots and sauté for 2 minutes without browning.

Add shrimp and sauté for 3 minutes or until just done. Add salt and pepper and toss well. Remove to a bowl, scraping in all the sauce.

Add lemon juice and dill; toss together well, cover, and refrigerate 3–4 hours before serving.

Serve with cocktail picks.

Serves 6–8 (unless you're a Craig, in which case it serves about 2)

SOUR CREAM, CAVIAR, LOX MOLD

1 envelope gelatin
$^1/_4$ cup cold water
$^1/_2$ cup heavy cream
8 oz. cream cheese, softened
1 cup sour cream
1 tbsp. Worcestershire sauce
Dash Tabasco sauce
2 tbsp. chives, chopped
1 tsp. lemon juice
1 tbsp. parsley, chopped
1 tbsp. prepared horseradish
$^1/_2$ lb. coarsely chopped Nova Scotia salmon (lox)*
4 oz. red caviar

Sometimes an occasion requires a little more fussing than usual. A food processor takes most of the time-consuming preparation out of this recipe, so you can be a star with little effort. A fish-shaped mold would add to the presentation of this dish, and fresh dill sprigs would make a nice garnish.

—Zee

Soak the gelatin in cold water, and then add the cream.

Combine the cream cheese and sour cream in a food processor or mixer.

Add the gelatin-cream mixture, the Worcestershire sauce, Tabasco, chives, lemon juice, parsley, and horseradish to the above and combine.

Blend in the salmon and caviar.

Rinse a 1-qt. mold with cold water and dry. Coat inside with vegetable oil. Fill with above mixture and chill, covered, for at least 12 hours.

When ready to serve, loosen edges with a sharp knife, cover bottom and sides of mold with a warm, damp towel, and place serving plate on top. Reverse mold and unmold contents onto plate. Serve with sliced black bread.

* **Note:** For something different, try substituting smoked bluefish for the lox.

TARAMOSALATA (Salted Fish Roe Dip)

6 slices white bread, crusts removed (or amount to achieve desired consistency)
$^1/_4$ cup taramosalata (salted fish roe) or red caviar
2 tbsp. freshly squeezed and strained lemon juice
2 tbsp. grated mild onion (like Vidalia)
$^1/_3$–$^1/_2$ cup extra virgin olive oil

We were introduced to this dish in Greece, where it's served as a starter course. These starters, or mezes *as they're known in the Middle East, are some of our favorite Mediterranean foods, and we've made many a meal out of only a selection of* mezes.

—Phil

Dip bread in water and squeeze dry.

Place roe (or caviar) in blender container with bread and blend until smooth. With motor running, add lemon juice and onion, and pour in olive oil in a slow, steady stream, using enough to make a rich, smooth texture. Chill.

Serve with crisp pita wedges or garlic Melba toast rounds and lemon wedges. Tiny shrimp and parsley sprigs may be used as a garnish.

Makes 1 cup

EGGS STUFFED WITH CAVIAR

8 hardboiled eggs
3 oz. softened cream cheese
2 tbsp. sour cream
2 tbsp. chives, snipped
3 tsp. red caviar

Slice eggs in half lengthwise. Carefully remove yolks and force through a sieve into a bowl. Blend in cream cheese, sour cream, and chives. Carefully fold in caviar. Chill mixture, covered, for 30 minutes. Fill the reserved halves with the mixture and garnish with more caviar. If filling will not fill all egg halves, mince the remaining halves and sprinkle around base of filled eggs.

Makes 12–16 stuffed eggs

A delish deviled egg variation. You might want to double this recipe.

—J.W.

CHILI-CHEESE BITES

1 (4-oz.) can chopped green chilies
4 cups grated Cheddar cheese
6 eggs, beaten
1 tbsp. finely chopped onion

Grease an 8x8″ baking pan. Spread chilies evenly over bottom. Sprinkle grated cheese over chilies. Add onion to beaten eggs and pour mixture over cheese. Bake in preheated oven at 350° for 30 minutes or until eggs are set. Cut into 1″ squares. Serve warm or at room temperature.

This dish is something like a crustless quiche. These bites have a Mexican air about them, and you might try them instead of nachos. I make these with jalapeños from our garden, but you may prefer the milder green chilies.

—Shirley

ELAINE'S CHICKEN WINGS

Elaine Patt made these wings, and they were the most sought-after contribution to our annual neighborhood gatherings. Elaine used to make a special container filled with wings just for Phil, who jealously guarded his stash, sharing his wings with nobody! He loves them hot or cold.

—Shirley

Chicken wings (the following marinade makes enough for about 5 lbs.)
1 cup soy sauce (Zee prefers lite soy sauce)
$\frac{1}{2}$ cup water
2–3 tsp. garlic powder, or to taste

Place chicken wings in large ziplock plastic bag. Mix marinade ingredients together and pour over chicken. Seal bag and shake to coat all of the wings. Refrigerate wings overnight, turning bag frequently so that all pieces are well marinated. (If you don't want to stay up all night, start wings marinating early in the day.)

Remove wings from marinade and place on foil-lined baking sheet. Bake in 350° preheated oven for 40 minutes, turning once.

SCALLOPS GRAVLOX (Gravlops?)

As with bluefish seviche, freshness is of ultimate importance. I prepare this dish in Off Season.

—J.W.

Place a single layer of scallops in the bottom of a glass baking dish. Cover with sprigs of fresh dill, $\frac{1}{4}$ cup sugar, and a bit of salt. Cover all with a plate weighted down by a brick (or old flatiron). Refrigerate for 48–72 hours. Serve as an appetizer with homemade French bread.

ARTICHOKE NIBBLERS

2 (6-oz.) jars marinated artichoke hearts
1 small onion, finely chopped
1 clove garlic, minced
4 eggs, beaten
$^1/_4$ cup fine, dry bread crumbs
$^1/_4$ tsp. salt
$^1/_8$ tsp. each: pepper, dried oregano, and Tabasco
$^1/_2$ lb. Cheddar cheese, grated
2 tbsp. dried parsley flakes
1 small jar of diced pimiento, drained

These nibblers are becoming popular, and justifiably so. They're another sort of crustless quiche. Your guests will want your recipe.

—J.W.

Drain liquid from 1 jar of artichoke hearts and discard. Drain about half of the liquid from the other jar into a frying pan. Sauté onion and garlic in the liquid. Chop artichokes into quarters, or smaller. Combine eggs, crumbs, and seasonings. Stir in cheese, pimiento, artichokes, and onion mixture. Pour into a buttered 7x11″ baking dish. Sprinkle with parsley. Bake at 325° for 30 minutes or until lightly set. Cool before cutting into 1″ squares. Serve warm or at room temperature.

"How can you govern a country that has 246 varieties of cheese?"
—Charles de Gaulle

SPINACH BALLS

2 pkgs. frozen, chopped spinach (cooked and well drained)
4 beaten eggs
2 cups herb stuffing mix
1 medium onion, chopped finely
1/2 cup melted butter
1/2 cup grated Parmesan cheese
1/2 tsp. dried thyme leaves
Dash of garlic powder

We are spinach fans and onion fans, and we enjoy and use all of the ingredients in this recipe, so it's no wonder we like the product. Shirl got the recipe from her mother.

—Phil

Mix all ingredients together. Chill mixture. Roll into 1″ balls and bake at 350° for 15 minutes. The balls may be frozen, separated on a cookie sheet, then bagged in plastic to thaw and bake later.

Serve warm.

Makes about 50 balls

ASPARAGUS ROLL-UPS

1 bunch asparagus, cooked crisp tender and trimmed to appropriate size
1 pkg. spreadable herbed cheese (like Alouette)
1/2 lb. thinly sliced deli ham

Simple and good. There are never any of these left over after a party. If you don't eat mammals, you can use turkey ham.

—Zee

Cut ham slices in half. Thinly spread each slice with cheese. Roll ham slice around asparagus spear.

Chill and serve.

DEEP-FRIED CAULIFLOWER

1 head of cauliflower
Milk
Flour
Vegetable oil
Salt and pepper to taste, or use other seasoning such as
curry or Cajun seasoning

Clean cauliflower and cut into bite-size flowerets. Dip
flowerets into milk to coat and dredge in seasoned flour,
shaking off excess flour. Deep fry in hot oil just until lightly
colored. Do not overcrowd pieces. Drain on paper towels
and keep hot until all cauliflower is fried.

Serve hot and pass the salt shaker for those who prefer
additional seasoning.

In The Woman Who
Walked into the Sea, *Phil wrote: "The only people who don't like fried cauliflower are the kind you really shouldn't hang around with anyway, since sooner or later they'll corrupt whatever good taste you have in other areas of your life as well." Even cauliflower haters love this recipe, served as an appetizer. And Phil likes it so much that he once fantasized about opening a restaurant called Phil's Phries, which would specialize in this dish.*

—Shirley

DOLMAS (Stuffed Vine Leaves)

1 lb. grape leaves (available in jars)
1 cup long-grain rice, uncooked
1 small to medium onion, finely chopped
$^1/_4$ cup fresh parsley, snipped
$^1/_4$ cup fresh dill, snipped
Salt and pepper to taste
$^1/_3$ cup piñon nuts
Dash of ground cinnamon
$^1/_3$ cup olive oil
Lemon

You can buy good canned dolmas, but J.W. and Zee like to make their own now and then. When they do, they sometimes use the young leaves of the wild grapes that gave the Vineyard its name. If you go that route, make sure you blanch the leaves until they're tender; otherwise, you'll be faced with some hard chewing!

—Shirley

Drain grape leaves (if using bottled leaves). Soak in hot water to cover for 20 minutes and drain in colander. Blanch fresh leaves in boiling water to cover for 5 minutes and drain again in colander. Refresh under cold water and pat dry with paper towels.

Sauté onion and piñon nuts in olive oil. Combine with remaining filling ingredients, except lemon.

Put 1 tbsp. of filling on the dull side of each leaf at the stem end. Fold up the sides and roll up the leaves, folding ends closed and squeezing lightly. Arrange rolls in 1 or 2 layers, seam side down, in large steamer. Add a small clove of garlic if desired, and drizzle with lemon juice.

Put water in bottom of steamer and steam, over boiling water, 1–2 hours or until leaves and rice are tender, adding water as necessary. Let cool and refrigerate until ready to serve. Serve with lemon wedges.

To serve hot, keep grape leaves warm and serve with Egg Lemon Sauce.

EGG LEMON SAUCE

2 eggs
3 tbsp. lemon juice
Salt and pepper to taste
1 cup broth reserved from steamer used to steam grape leaves

Separate eggs. Beat egg whites to stiff peaks. Beat yolks, in separate bowl, until light and lemon colored. Fold egg whites into yolks. Slowly stir in lemon juice. Gradually add reserved broth to egg mixture. Cook and stir over low heat until slightly thickened and smooth (about 5 minutes). Season to taste with salt and pepper.

Do not boil sauce.

ELAINE'S CHEESE MELTS

1 cup finely grated Parmesan cheese (fresh is best)
1 cup mayonnaise
1/2 cup very finely chopped red onion
1 loaf small party rye bread

Mix first three ingredients and spread on rye bread slices. Bake in preheated 400° oven just until browned and bubbly (about 10 minutes). Watch carefully to prevent overbrowning.

If you keep a loaf of party rye bread in your freezer, you'll probably have the other ingredients already on hand and can whip these up at the arrival of unexpected guests.

—Shirley

HERBED EGGPLANT SLICES

4 tbsp. extra virgin olive oil

1 clove garlic, crushed

1 eggplant (about 1½ lbs.), trimmed, peeled, and cut into ½"-thick slices

½ tsp. fresh rosemary leaves, chopped

½ tsp. fresh thyme leaves, chopped

½ tsp. fresh oregano leaves, chopped

¼ tsp. salt

Freshly ground black pepper

1–2 tbsp. red wine vinegar

While traveling in Greece and Turkey, we learned to love regional eggplant dishes, especially many appetizers. This is a typical hors d'oeuvre. Imagine yourself sitting at a table overlooking the Mediterranean. It's a sunny day and you're having wine and herbed eggplant slices. Because eggplant is a member of the nightshade family, you may think you've died and gone to heaven!

—Shirley and Phil

Combine half of the oil and the garlic in small bowl. Lightly brush eggplant slices with mixture. Arrange slices in single layer on nonstick baking sheet. Combine herbs and salt in small bowl. Sprinkle herb mix evenly over eggplant slices. Grind some black pepper over all.

Bake in preheated 425° oven until browned and tender (about 10 minutes). Brush with additional oil if necessary.

Whisk remaining oil and vinegar together until well blended, and sprinkle on eggplant slices. Serve warm or at room temperature with crisped pita bread wedges or thin slices of crusty bread.

Serves 4–6 as an appetizer

MUSHROOMS IN GARLIC SAUCE

³/₄ lb. mushrooms, trimmed, cleaned (and halved or
quartered if large)
4¹/₂ tbsp. olive oil
3 medium cloves garlic, finely chopped
2¹/₄ tbsp. flour
1¹/₂ cups beef (or chicken) broth
³/₄ dried hot red chili pepper, seeded and cut into 4 pieces
3 tbsp. parsley, finely chopped
3 tsp. freshly squeezed and strained lemon juice
Salt to taste

*We love mushrooms in
all forms. This recipe is a
nice change from stuffed
mushrooms, and very
easy to do.*

—Zee

In medium-sized, heavy skillet, heat 3 tbsp. of the oil over
medium-high heat. Add the garlic and sauté, stirring, until
barely colored (not too brown). Remove pan from heat and
stir in flour until smooth. Return to heat and cook, stirring,
1–2 minutes. Gradually stir in broth. Add chili pepper, one-
half of the parsley, lemon juice, and salt; cook, stirring,
until sauce is thick and smooth. Remove from heat and
set aside.

In medium-sized, heavy skillet, heat the remaining oil over
high heat. Add mushrooms and sauté, stirring frequently,
until they are lightly browned. Add the mushrooms to the
sauce and simmer 5 minutes.

Adjust seasonings, if necessary, and transfer to heated
serving bowl. Sprinkle with remaining parsley and serve
immediately.

Serves 6

ELAINE'S BRUSCHETTA

Another recipe J.W. stole from Elaine Patt and plans to keep. An excellent munchie with cocktails. Make this dish when the plum tomatoes are plentiful.

—Phil

1 cup chopped parsley
$^{1}/_{2}$ cup chopped red onion
$^{1}/_{4}$ cup chopped, seeded tomato
8 finely diced anchovy fillets (optional)
1 tbsp. chopped garlic
$^{1}/_{4}$ cup olive oil
2 tbsp. red wine or balsamic vinegar
1 tsp. dried oregano

Mix all ingredients together and store, covered, in glass container in the refrigerator. Serve on bruschetta or toast rounds with additional olive oil for drizzling.

WARM ARTICHOKE DIP

Oooohhhh, if only we could grow artichokes in our garden. This is scrumptious!

—Zee

1 can artichoke hearts, drained and mashed
$^{1}/_{2}$ cup mayonnaise
8 oz. cream cheese
6 oz. shredded Mozzarella cheese
1 cup grated Parmesan cheese
$^{1}/_{8}$ tsp. garlic powder

Mix all ingredients together and pour into small earthenware bowl. Bake at 350° for 15 minutes or until hot and bubbly. Serve with toasted pita bread.

This mixture can also be spread on individual rounds of bread and toasted.

RED PEPPER BRUSCHETTA WITH FETA CHEESE

1 (7-oz.) jar roasted red peppers, drained and chopped
4 oz. finely crumbled Feta cheese
1/4 cup chopped green onions
1 clove garlic, minced
Olive oil
1 tsp. lemon juice
1 loaf French bread, cut into 1/2" slices

Mix together peppers, cheese, onions, garlic, 1 tbsp. olive oil, and lemon juice; set aside.

Brush bread slices lightly with additional olive oil. Place on cookie sheet and broil on each side until lightly toasted. Watch closely to prevent burning.

Top each slice with about 1 tbsp. of red pepper mixture or serve mixture in a bowl surrounded with toast slices.

Makes about 18 individual servings

While you're waiting for the tomatoes to ripen, you won't be disappointed with this delicious alternative to the previous recipe. It's my favorite!

—Zee

SUSIE'S NIBBLIES

2 lbs. salted mixed nuts
12 oz. Wheat Chex cereal
10½ oz. Cheerios
10½ oz. Rice Chex cereal
6½ oz. thin pretzel sticks (broken into smaller pieces)
2 cups canola oil
2 tbsp. Worcestershire sauce
1 tbsp. garlic powder
1 tbsp. seasoned salt

Susie Rowland made these nibblies first. Now Zee and Shirley do. They usually serve them during the Thanksgiving-Christmas holiday season. They store them in jars and canisters while they last, which isn't long.

—Phil

Mix first 5 ingredients together in very large, high-sided roasting pan. Mix remaining 4 ingredients together well and pour over cereal mixture. Stir well. Bake in preheated 250° oven for 2 hours, stirring every 20 minutes. Spread on absorbent paper toweling to cool before storing. This recipe makes enough to share with friends. When packaged in attractive jars or boxes, it makes a nice hostess or holiday gift.

REFRIED BEAN DIP

1 cup salsa
1 (16-oz.) can refried beans
1–2 tbsp. chopped fresh cilantro
$\frac{1}{2}$ lb. grated Monterey jack cheese
$\frac{1}{4}$ cup sliced jalapeno peppers (or to taste)

Mix salsa and half of the cheese with the refried beans.
Divide mixture between 2 shallow (7$\frac{1}{2}$" diameter) earthenware dishes. Spread remaining cheese on top of each.
Garnish with sliced peppers. Microwave for 3 minutes or
until warmed through, or heat in 375° oven for 10–12
minutes. Serve with tortilla chips.

*This is our favorite
version of this standby
because of the ease of
preparation and the
good results. It's easy to
take to a gathering
where it can readily be
heated in a microwave.*

—Zee

CHRIS'S BEAN DIP

2 (15-oz.) cans of kidney beans, drained and rinsed
$\frac{1}{3}$ medium onion, chopped finely
1 garlic clove, minced
$\frac{1}{3}$ cup mayonnaise
$\frac{1}{3}$ cup sweet relish
Dash of dry mustard
Salt and pepper to taste

Mix all ingredients together and refrigerate for several
hours. Serve with tortilla chips.

*I got this excellent recipe
from Christina Taylor,
the Greek bombshell. It
makes a dip that you
can't stop eating! The
recipe first appeared in
A Fatal Vineyard Season.*

—J.W.

WASABI DIP

2 tbsp. wasabi powder
$1/2$ cup good mayonnaise
$1/2$ cup dairy sour cream
$1/4$ tsp. Dijon mustard
Pinch salt

Phil and I first had this at a gathering of the Island Community Chorus, as a dip for sugar snap peas. It is addictive and does justice to those delectable edible pod peas fresh from the garden.

—Shirley

Mix wasabi powder in enough water to make a smooth paste. Let stand 10 minutes. Whisk other ingredients in another bowl. Add small amount of wasabi paste and mix until very smooth. Add remaining wasabi paste and mix well.

This is a great dip served with asparagus spears or sugar snap peas (cooked until crisp tender), tuna (or other firm fish), chicken, or beef, and with any Asian meal.

Keeps refrigerated for at least a week.

TZATZIKI (A Greek Appetizer)

1 quart yogurt (whole milk variety)
2 large cucumbers, peeled, seeded, and grated
½–1 tsp. salt
1–2 large cloves of garlic, minced
⅛ tsp. white pepper
1–2 tbsp. olive oil
1–2 tbsp. fresh dill, parsley, or cilantro, chopped (optional)

Empty the yogurt into a yogurt strainer or a colander lined with a double thickness of dampened cheesecloth, paper towels, or a large coffee filter, set on a bowl. Cover with plastic wrap and let drain at room temperature for 2 or more hours, or refrigerate for up to 12 hours, until yogurt is thick and custardy and 1½ cups of liquid have been collected in bowl. Discard liquid.

This is a very refreshing accompaniment to many traditional Middle Eastern dishes.

—Phil

Place grated cucumbers in a sieve over a bowl and sprinkle with ½–1 tsp. salt. Toss and set aside to drain for at least 30 minutes.

Transfer drained yogurt to a mixing bowl and add garlic, pepper, and ½ tbsp. olive oil. Mix well.

Press down on grated cucumber in sieve with the back of a spoon until as much of the juice as possible has been extracted. Add drained cucumber to yogurt mixture, mix well, and refrigerate for at least 1 hour before serving.

If desired, mix in some chopped herbs before serving, and drizzle a little olive oil over the top.

Serve as an appetizer salad or as an hors d'oeuvre with pita bread or crudités.

Makes about 3 cups

DONNA'S MUSHROOM BUNDLES

2 doz. (1″ or smaller) mushrooms
¼ cup chive-and-onion cream cheese (or your favorite herb-flavored cream cheese)
one-half of a 17¼ oz. pkg. of frozen puff pastry, thawed
1 egg, slightly beaten

These delectable morsels will disappear before your very eyes. They can be made ahead of time (up to about 12 hours) and refrigerated, covered. Brush with the egg wash just before baking.

—J.W.

Preheat oven to 400°. Remove stems from mushrooms, and fill each cap with ½ tsp. of the cream cheese mixture.

Roll puff pastry, on lightly floured surface, to a 15x10″ rectangle. Cut into 24 (2½″) squares.

For each bundle, place a filled mushroom in the center of a pastry square. Draw up the 4 corners to form a small bundle and firmly pinch the edges to form a small knob at the top. Place on ungreased cookie sheet, and brush each bundle with a little of the beaten egg.

Bake for 12–15 minutes or until golden. Cool 5 minutes before serving.

Serves 6

PARTY PLATTER PINWHEELS

8 oz. cream cheese (softened)
2 tbsp. mayonnaise
4 oz. diced green chilies (or jalapenos), canned or fresh—be
sure to drain canned chilies
1 large tomato, seeded and chopped finely
$1/4$ cup finely diced onion
1 clove garlic, minced
1 tsp. chili powder
$1/2$ tsp. salt
Flour tortillas (use the large ones to speed up preparation)

Blend cream cheese with mayonnaise and stir in remaining
ingredients. Cover and refrigerate for a couple of hours,
then spread mixture over tortillas and roll up tightly. Trim
the ends of each tortilla, and wrap rolls in plastic wrap.
Refrigerate until firm, then slice into $1/2''$ slices and place
on cookie sheet. Broil until lightly golden.

These make an easy and tasty addition to a party platter. You may also use the filling as a dip for taco chips.

—Zee

Soups and Chowders

"HAPPINESS IS HAVING CHOWDER IN
YOUR FRIDGE WAITING TO BE HEATED."

—J.W., IN *MURDER AT A VINEYARD MANSION*

NEW ENGLAND CLAM CHOWDER

1 large onion
4 slices of bacon (or equivalent amount of diced salt pork)
2 cups diced potatoes
24 large quahogs (hard-shelled New England clams)
1 quart milk (may use part half-and-half)
$1/4$ tsp. freshly ground black pepper

Hold the tomatoes! New Englanders do not use tomatoes in their clam chowder! This recipe is made by J.W. in Off Season *and* Death on a Vineyard Beach, *and the recipe may be found at the back of* Vineyard Shadows.

—Phil

Dice bacon and onions and fry together until onion is golden and translucent. Add 2 cups of diced potatoes, and cover all with water. Boil until potatoes are tender but firm. While this is cooking, steam the clams (use more than 24 if you have extras) just until they open. Chop quahog meat coarsely in food processor, by hand, or by meat grinder. Add quahogs and steaming broth (if not too salty, in which case you should dilute with plain water) to potato mixture. Immediately add milk and ground pepper. Bring only to a simmer but do not boil.

Chowder may be thickened by adding a mixture of 1 tbsp. flour mixed with $1/4$ cup milk. Simmer about 10 minutes after adding thickening. Serve piping hot with a dab of butter and oyster crackers.

Note: Chowder base (before milk is added) may be frozen. The texture of the potatoes will change somewhat, but no flavor will be lost.

You can also freeze the quahogs raw in the shell or removed from the shell after steaming. The latter saves space in your freezer.

Serves 4–6

KALE SOUP

1 shin bone of beef (or marrow bones)
1 lb. beef chuck, cubed, shaken in a bag of seasoned flour, and braised
1 (10–12″) piece of kielbasa, parboiled and sliced
1 envelope (1-oz.) dry onion soup mix for each 4–5 cups liquid
2 large onions, coarsely chopped
2 (10-oz.) pkgs. frozen kale, chopped (or fresh equivalent)
1 (1-lb.) can kidney beans (or chili beans)
2–3 large new potatoes*, diced (or about 8 oz. macaroni)
2–3 tsp. pesto or 2 tsp. dried basil
1 tbsp. chili powder (or to taste)
Salt or seasoned salt and pepper to taste

My mother was of Azorean descent, and this soup was a staple in our home when I was growing up. I think every Portuguese family cooks its own version, and the recipe mutates with every generation. This is my version. I always cook a large vat so that I can have the security of a stash in the freezer. The recipe was previously printed in A Vineyard Killing.

—Shirley

Place shin bone of beef in large Dutch oven and cover with cold water. Bring to a boil. Add braised beef and simmer until tender (1–2 hours), adding water if necessary. Remove meat and marrow from bone and return to pot. Add soup mix, onions and kale, and additional water or stock as required. Simmer for 15–20 minutes, until kale is nearly tender. Add sliced kielbasa, potatoes, seasonings, and pesto. Add kidney beans when potatoes are nearly done. Add pasta, if using, during last 10 minutes. (See package cooking times.) Any other cooked leftover vegetables (such as corn, carrots, rice, etc.) may be added at this time. Season with salt and pepper to taste.

Serve hot with a sprinkling of grated Jack or Cheddar cheese, and crusty bread.

If you decide to freeze this soup, you may prefer to add boiled potatoes after thawing the soup, as the texture of the potatoes, although not the flavor, will change if frozen.

MOSTLY VEGETABLE SOUP

This looks like a long recipe (a sous chef makes it easier), but it goes together very easily and is a good way to clean out the refrigerator. I believe that most soups should be made in large batches so that portions can be frozen for an easy meal later on, or shared with friends.

—Shirley

2–3 tbsp. olive oil

Chicken stock (preferably homemade)—about 12 cups

2 pkgs. dry onion soup mix

2 leeks, sliced thinly

4–5 ribs celery, sliced

1–2 sweet green or red peppers cut in large dice

3 Portobello mushroom caps, cut in large dice (or 10 oz. sliced white mushrooms)

1/4 small cabbage (red or green or combination), shredded

4 carrots, peeled and sliced

2 10-oz. pkgs. chopped frozen kale or spinach

1 cup dry lentils, cooked

1 can white northern beans

1 can whole kernel corn

1–2 cups frozen, cubed butternut squash (if desired, for added flavor)

2–4 cups cooked spiral pasta

Chicken pieces from carcass

1/2 lb. sliced turkey kielbasa

Herbes de Provence, to taste

Minced garlic (2–3 cloves)

1 tbsp. chili powder

Dona Flora's Bean Supreme*

Salt and pepper to taste

1 tbsp. basil pesto (if desired)

In large Dutch oven, sauté leeks, celery, green peppers, and carrots in olive oil for about 15 minutes or until somewhat tender. Add mushrooms and sauté 10 more minutes. Pour in about 8 cups of the chicken stock and add the cabbage, kale, and onion soup mix. Bring to a boil, cover, and simmer for 15–20 minutes. Add remaining ingredients, except cooked pasta. Add additional stock as necessary. Add seasonings and continue to simmer until vegetables are tender but not mushy. Add pasta and heat, if necessary, before serving. Serve in bowls and pass shredded Cheddar (smoked Cheddar adds a nice flavor) or Jack cheese to sprinkle on top.

Serves a large crowd but also freezes well. A stash in the freezer gives a great sense of security during a cold winter.

Note: All seasoning amounts are approximate and can be adjusted to taste. Stock amounts are also approximate, depending on how thick you want your soup. Jeff and Zee like a soup of almost stew consistency. Of course, any leftover veggies may be added.

Dona Flora's Bean Supreme can be ordered from: Dona Flora, P.O. Box 7, Laconner, WA 98257.

Of soup and love, the first is best.
—SPANISH PROVERB (NOTE: ZEE DISAGREES.)

CREAM OF REFRIGERATOR SOUP
(Green Vichyssoise)

3 leeks (white part), washed and thinly sliced

1 large onion, thinly sliced

2 oz. spinach, washed and shredded

Any other leftover veggies (except maybe beets)

2 tbsp. unsalted butter or margarine

3 cups chicken broth

2 medium potatoes, peeled and diced

1 cup milk, scalded

$^1/_2$ tsp. salt

Dash white pepper

$^1/_2$ cup heavy cream (J.W. actually uses skimmed milk, and finds it just as good)

Chopped chives

This soup is never made quite the same way twice because you rarely have the same leftovers in your refrigerator. It may be served hot or cold; I prefer it cold. The recipe appeared in Vineyard Blues.

—J.W.

Sauté leek, onion, and spinach in butter in large saucepan for 20 minutes, stirring occasionally, until soft but not brown. Add any other leftover vegetables.

Stir in chicken broth and potatoes; cook 20 minutes longer or until potatoes are tender. Add milk; bring mixture just to boiling and remove from heat. Add seasonings to taste. Puree soup through food mill or in food processor. Chill several hours.

Stir cream into chilled soup. Serve in chilled cups with a sprinkling of chopped chives.

SHERRIED BLACK BEAN SOUP

$^1/_2$ cup thinly sliced carrots

1 small onion, chopped

2 stalks thinly sliced celery

1 cup frozen or canned corn kernels

1–2 cups cooked spiral pasta (optional)

4 cloves garlic, minced

1 tbsp. olive oil

2 tsp. ground cumin

2 15-oz. cans black beans, rinsed and drained

1 cup sliced turkey kielbasa

$^1/_4$ cup dry sherry

1 tsp. instant chicken bouillon granules

2 bay leaves

1 tsp. dried oregano, crushed

$^1/_8$ tsp. ground red pepper

$^1/_4$ cup dairy sour cream

This is one of my favorite soups, and I confess to usually doubling the recipe. Many soups may be made with only a small amount of meat or no meat at all. This is one of them.

—Zee

In a 3-qt. Dutch oven, sauté carrots, onion, celery, and garlic in hot oil over medium-low heat for about 3 minutes. Add cumin and cook until carrots are tender. Stir in 4 cups water, beans, kielbasa, sherry, bouillon granules, bay leaves, oregano, and ground red pepper. Bring to boiling and reduce heat.

Simmer uncovered for 15 minutes. Add corn kernels and continue to cook for 10 minutes. Remove bay leaves and add cooked pasta (if using). Ladle into bowls and top with sour cream.

Serves 4

TONI'S RUSSIAN CURRY SOUP

1 can split-pea soup (undiluted)
$^1/_2$ can tomato soup (undiluted)
$1^1/_2$ soup cans milk
$^1/_2$ soup can cream
$^3/_4$ tsp. curry powder

What could be easier as a part of a soup-and-sandwich lunch? You don't need a vat to make this either. We got the recipe from good cook and friend Toni Chute.

—Shirley

Heat all ingredients and serve with dollop of sour cream and fresh croutons.

Serves 2

CREAM OF PEANUT SOUP

1 cup natural peanut butter (oil poured off)
3 cups chicken stock
1 cup stale beer
1 tbsp. cayenne pepper
$^1/_2$ cup hot green chili peppers, minced
1 cup light cream

Don't knock it 'til you've tried it. It is a natural for peanut butter fans, and Jimmy Carter probably approves of it!

—Phil

Combine all ingredients except cream in blender, and blend until smooth. Heat over low heat just until bubbly. Add cream, re-warm, and serve.

Serves 2

PEANUT AND PUMPKIN SOUP

4 medium onions, chopped
6 shallots, finely chopped ($^1/_2$ cup)
4 cloves garlic, finely minced
1 tsp. leaf marjoram, crumbled
$^1/_2$ tsp. thyme leaves, crumbled
$^1/_4$ tsp. grated nutmeg
3 tbsp. peanut or vegetable oil
1 (13$^3/_4$ oz.) can chicken broth
1 (13$^3/_4$ oz.) can beef broth (or use all chicken broth)
1 (29 oz.) can pumpkin puree (not pie mix)
1 cup creamy peanut butter
2 cups milk
2 cups half-and-half
1 tsp. liquid red pepper seasoning
$^1/_2$ cup coarsely chopped dry-roasted peanuts or toasted
pumpkin seeds (for garnish)

This is a bit more work than Cream of Peanut Soup, but is delicious and worth the little extra effort. It makes a great addition to a harvest festival meal.

—Shirley

Sauté onion, shallot, garlic, and seasonings in oil in large saucepan or Dutch oven for 5 minutes or until golden. Reduce heat to low, cover, and cook 25 minutes or until limp.

Add broths. Simmer, covered, 20 minutes. Cool 15 minutes. In batches, puree in food processor or blender.

Return mixture to pan. Stir in pumpkin, peanut butter, milk, cream, and red pepper seasoning. Bring to a simmer over moderate heat. Serve immediately or chill (tightly covered) until shortly before serving. Reheat over moderately low heat for about 10 minutes or serve cold.

Garnish with chopped peanuts or pumpkin seeds.

Serves 8–10

SWEET POTATO SOUP

2 tbsp. butter
1 cup onion, chopped
2 small celery stalks, chopped (reserve leaves for garnish)
1 medium leek, sliced (white and light green parts)
1 large clove garlic, chopped
1½ lb. red-skinned sweet potatoes (yams), peeled and cut into 1" cubes (about 5 cups)
4 cups chicken stock
1 cinnamon stick
¼ tsp. ground nutmeg
1½ cups half-and-half
2 tbsp. pure maple syrup

This is a winter solstice favorite at the Jackson house. The soup may be made ahead and frozen (before the half-and-half and maple syrup are added). It is a spot of sunshine on the shortest day of the year.

—J.W.

Melt butter in large heavy pot over medium-high heat. Sauté onion in butter for 5 minutes. Add celery and leeks and sauté until onion is translucent (about 5 minutes). Add garlic and sauté 2 minutes. Add potatoes, stock, and spices. Bring to a boil, reduce heat and simmer, uncovered, until potatoes are tender (about 20 minutes). Remove cinnamon stick. Puree soup in blender (in batches). Return soup to pot and add half-and-half and maple syrup. Season with salt and pepper. Serve hot, sprinkled with chopped celery leaves or Fried Sage Leaves (see page 180).

Serves 6 as a first course

GAZPACHO

1 small onion
2 cloves garlic
3 green peppers, seeded
4 tomatoes, peeled and seeded
1 cucumber, peeled and seeded
Salt and pepper to taste
$\frac{1}{2}$ tsp. chili powder
$\frac{1}{3}$ cup olive oil
3 cups tomato juice
$\frac{1}{4}$ cup lemon juice
$\frac{1}{4}$ cup dry sherry
$\frac{1}{2}$ cup sour cream

This refreshing Spanish vegetable soup is best served icy cold. A food processor makes it easy.

—Phil

Chop vegetables in food processor until finely chopped. Mix in other ingredients and chill. Serve cold with a dollop of sour cream.

Serves 6

*"Beautiful soup, so rich and green,
waiting in a hot tureen!
Who for such dainties would not stoop!
Soup of the evening, beautiful soup!"*
—LEWIS CARROLL, *ALICE IN WONDERLAND*

AVGOLEMONO (Egg/Lemon Soup)

2 qts. chicken broth
$1/2$ cup long grain rice (or orzo)
Salt and pepper to taste
5 eggs, beaten
$1/4$–$1/2$ cup fresh lemon juice (to your liking)
1 tbsp. flour

Bring broth to boil in medium saucepan. Add rice and simmer, covered, for 20 minutes (10 minutes for orzo). Add salt and pepper.

Serve this as the first course for a Greek meal. Be sure to add the lemon juice gradually and to taste the soup before adding more. This is a simple but delectable soup.

—Shirley

Combine eggs, lemon juice, and flour. Blend thoroughly.

Slowly add 1 cup hot broth to egg mixture, stirring well. Add egg mixture to broth in saucepan, stirring constantly, and cook over low heat for about 5 minutes. Do not boil.

Serves 6

VERMONT CHEDDAR SOUP

3 qts. chicken stock
1 small onion, chopped
2 cloves garlic, minced
5 oz. butter
6 oz. flour
2 cups half-and-half
1 cup heavy cream
1+ tsp. fresh thyme, finely chopped
2 bay leaves
Salt
Pepper, freshly ground
1 lb. Vermont sharp or extra sharp Cheddar cheese, grated
1 cup carrots, grated
1 cup celery, minced

This splendid recipe was given to J.W. by Simon Pearce. To eat Simon's own soup, you go to his place in Quechee Gorge, Vermont.

—Zee

Bring stock to boil. Melt butter in heavy stock pot, add onions and garlic; soften. Add flour to butter and onion mixture. Stir to combine well, turn heat very low. Stirring occasionally, cook about 15 minutes. Add stock 1/3 at a time. Stir with whisk until smooth. Season with thyme, bay leaves, salt, and pepper. Cook over low heat until smooth and creamy. Add grated cheese. Boil water in separate sauce pan, and cook celery and carrots until just tender. Drain well. Add cooked celery-carrot mixture to stock pot. Add half-and-half and heavy cream. Stir well, gently heat, and serve.

PEAR-BRIE SOUP

2 small, ripe pears (about 3/4 lb.), peeled, halved, cored, and chopped
1/8 tsp. ground ginger
1/8 tsp. cinnamon
1/8 tsp. ground cloves
2 cups chicken broth
2 tbsp. unsalted butter or margarine
2 tbsp. flour
5 oz. can (2/3 cup) evaporated milk
4 oz. Brie, well chilled, rind removed, and cut into small cubes
Nutmeg

We love both pears and brie, so naturally we love this soup! So will you.

—Zee

In medium saucepan, combine first 4 ingredients with 1 cup of broth; mix well. Bring to a boil, reduce heat, cover and simmer 15–20 minutes (5 minutes if using canned pears) or until pears are tender. Puree mixture in food processor. Set aside.

Melt butter, or oleo, in heavy saucepan over medium heat. Whisk in flour. Add remaining broth, cook, and stir for 1 more minute. Gradually whisk in evaporated milk. Add cheese and whisk until smooth. Stir in pear puree. You can do this much ahead and refrigerate, covered, until just before serving time.

Heat gently (do not boil). Sprinkle with nutmeg before serving.

Makes 8 (1/2 cup) servings

LEEK AND POTATO SOUP

1 lb. leeks, white and tender green parts only, washed well
and chopped
1½ lb. red bliss or Yukon gold potatoes, peeled and chopped
1 tsp. dried dill
4 stalks celery, chopped
8 cups chicken broth
1 cup skim milk
Salt and white pepper to taste
Chopped chives for garnish

In large stock pot, over medium-high heat, bring first 5
ingredients to a simmer.

Reduce heat to medium and gently simmer for 30 minutes
or until potatoes are tender. Remove from heat and cool
before pureeing in a food processor or food mill. When
entire soup is pureed, pour back into stock pot, add milk,
and adjust seasonings with salt and pepper. Bring to simmer
again before serving. If serving cold, add milk and serve
immediately, or refrigerate until serving time.

Garnish with chopped chives and perhaps a chive blossom.

Serves 6–8

*Vichyssoise can be eaten
hot, but is typically
eaten cold. There are a
lot of minor and a few
major variations in the
recipes. This is one of
those recipes, and it's a
good one.*

—J.W.

MARTY'S CORN CHOWDER

4 strips bacon, fried crisp and crumbled
1 medium onion, finely chopped
2 cups fresh or frozen corn
2¹/₂ cups milk
2 tbsp. bacon drippings
1 cup cooked potatoes, diced
1 can cream of mushroom soup (undiluted)
Salt and pepper to taste

Phil's sister, Martha Walker, makes this delicious chowder out in Colorado. It tastes so rich that you think it must be loaded with cream and butter, but it isn't!

—Shirley

Sauté onion in bacon drippings; add corn, potatoes, and remaining ingredients. Heat and serve.

Serves 4

Salads and
Salad Dressings

"GARDENS ARE TERRIFIC.
GOD WAS PRETTY VINDICTIVE WHEN HE
THREW ADAM AND EVE OUT OF THEIRS.
NO WONDER THERE ARE SO MANY
PEOPLE MAD AT HER."

—J.W., IN *A VINEYARD KILLING*

SMOKED BLUEFISH SALAD

8 oz. smoked bluefish (deboned and flaked)
$^1/_4$–$^1/_2$ cup diced celery
Diced red onion to taste (or 1 tbsp. chopped chives)
1 tsp. Dijon mustard
$^1/_4$ cup mayonnaise
Salt and pepper to taste

J.W. makes a sandwich out of this salad in A Beautiful Place to Die. You might like to try it yourself, topped with a slice of horseradish-flavored Cheddar cheese, then grilled as you would a cheese sandwich.

—Phil

Lightly combine all ingredients and serve on Bibb lettuce or in sandwiches.

This salad can also be made with unsmoked, leftover cooked bluefish.

Many of these salads can be served as luncheon dishes, with crusty bread.

THAI SHRIMP AND NOODLE SALAD

1 lb. medium-size raw shrimp
8 oz. linguini
1 cup red bell pepper, cut into thin strips
$^1/_2$ cup fresh cilantro, chopped
$^1/_2$ cup scallions, diagonally sliced

Dressing:
$^1/_4$ cup chicken broth
3 tbsp. fresh lime juice
2 tbsp. reduced-sodium soy sauce
2 tbsp. dark Oriental sesame oil
$1^1/_2$ tsp. granulated sugar
$^3/_4$ tsp. ground ginger
$^1/_4$–$^1/_2$ tsp. crushed red pepper

When we traveled in Southeast Asia, we grew fonder than ever of the cuisine of the region. This is a light and refreshing luncheon dish that reminds us of that ancient, beautiful part of the world.

—Shirley and Phil

Cook shrimp in 1″ of simmering water, stirring often, 3–5 minutes until pink, firm, and opaque. Drain in colander and cool under running cold water. Peel and devein shrimp.

Meanwhile, cook linguini (according to package directions), adding bell pepper to pot 2 minutes before pasta is done. Drain in colander and cool under running cold water. Drain well.

Whisk dressing ingredients in serving bowl until blended. Stir in cilantro. Add linguini, shrimp, and scallions. Toss well. Cover and refrigerate at least 1 hour (or overnight) to blend flavors.

Serves 4

CILANTRO/LIME/CRAB SALAD IN AVOCADO HALVES

1/3 cup red onion, finely chopped

3 tbsp. mayonnaise

2 tbsp. fresh cilantro, chopped

3 tsp. fresh lime juice (use 2 tsp. in dressing and remainder to brush on avocado halves)

1/2 tsp. ground cumin

1/2 tsp. grated lime peel

8 oz. crabmeat

1 ripe avocado, halved, pitted, and peeled

Salt and pepper to taste

Lime wedges

How can you go wrong with a salad that includes avocado and crabmeat?

—J.W.

Stir first 6 ingredients together. Add crabmeat and season with salt and pepper.

Brush avocado halves with remaining lime juice. Arrange avocado halves, cut side up, on serving plates. Mound crab salad on each half. Serve with lime wedges.

Note: To complete as luncheon entrée, serve with tomato slices drizzled with balsamic vinaigrette and fresh cornbread.

Serves 2

CURRIED CHICKEN SALAD

Dressing:

Stir together:

$^{1}/_{2}$ cup mayonnaise

$^{1}/_{2}$ tsp. garlic powder

1 tsp. curry powder

$^{1}/_{8}$ tsp. cayenne pepper

$^{1}/_{2}$ tsp. prepared mustard

2 tsp. lemon juice

2 tbsp. finely chopped chutney (mango or Apricot Chutney is good) (see page 185)

Add and mix in:

$3^{1}/_{2}$ cups cooked, diced chicken

$^{2}/_{3}$ cup thinly sliced celery

2 thinly sliced scallions

1 small apple, cored and diced

This is our favorite chicken salad recipe, and it's so easy to prepare. A roasted chicken from the deli makes it even easier.

—Zee

Refrigerate salad and serve on a bed of greens (Boston-type lettuce leaves are good).

Serves 4 as a luncheon dish

MIDDLE EASTERN CHICKEN SALAD

1 long, seedless English cucumber
1/2 cup olive-flavored hummus (or any flavor you prefer)
1/4 cup fresh lemon juice
2 curried chicken breasts (see note), thinly sliced
1 can (about 15 oz.) chick peas (drained and rinsed)
4 cups packed spinach leaves, cut in narrow strips
1 cup grape (or cherry) tomatoes, cut in half
Sandwich-size pitas (whole wheat is good)

You may have noticed our fondness for Middle Eastern fare. This recipe could make you a convert.

—Shirley and Phil

Finely chop cucumber and transfer to a strainer. Press out excess liquid. Place in large bowl and stir in remaining ingredients, except pitas. Toss well. Warm pitas in oven or on grill. Cut open one end of pita and stuff pocket with chicken salad.

Serves 4

Note: Curried chicken breasts can be made by rubbing skinless breasts with a mixture of:

3/4 tbsp. curry powder
1 tsp. each of ground ginger and garlic powder
1/2 tsp. each of ground cinnamon and salt

Grill or broil chicken for 3–4 minutes per side or until cooked through. Cool and chill before adding to salad. Or use leftovers from Easy Curried Chicken (see page 120).

SPINACH SALAD

1 lb. fresh spinach leaves, washed, dried, and torn into
bite-sized pieces
2 scallions, sliced thinly (white and light green portions only)
3 strips bacon, cooked and crumbled
1 hard boiled egg, chopped
6 oz. mushrooms, sliced (optional)

*An old standby, but
always good. Popeye
would approve.*

—J.W.

Toss above ingredients with an Italian-type garlic-herb
dressing or a honey mustard dressing.

Serves 4

ORANGE/AVOCADO/RED ONION SALAD

Mixed spring greens
Orange slices (rind and seeds removed)
Avocado slices
Red onion, very thinly sliced

*We serve this salad often
to accompany chicken or
fish entrées. Canned
mandarin oranges,
drained and rinsed, may
be substituted, but fresh
oranges are best. Slice
the onion very thinly.*

—Shirley

Arrange orange, avocado, and onion slices over a bed of
mixed greens, either in individual salad bowls or large salad
bowl. Lightly dress with poppy seed dressing just before
serving.

Recipe amounts depend upon number of servings desired.

SPINACH WITH SHIITAKE MUSHROOMS

10 oz. baby spinach (or regular spinach well trimmed and deveined)

1/4 cup pine nuts (toasted)

Salt and pepper to taste

1 tsp. sugar

3 tbsp. balsamic vinegar

6 tbsp. olive oil

1 clove garlic, chopped

1/2 lb. shiitake mushrooms, trimmed and sliced

4 oz. goat cheese, crumbled

When you crave something a bit more exotic than the usual spinach salad, give this one a try. It is a palate pleaser. Some good breadsticks are a nice accompaniment.

—Zee

Heap spinach in a large bowl and sprinkle with nuts.

In another bowl, whisk salt, pepper, sugar, and vinegar together. Slowly drizzle in 4 tbsp. olive oil, and whisk until dressing emulsifies.

In large skillet, heat remaining olive oil, and add garlic, mushrooms, and a pinch of salt. Cover and cook over medium-low heat for about 10 minutes or until softened. Uncover and continue to cook until lightly golden in color. Remove from heat and add to spinach.

Pour dressing over salad and toss well. Sprinkle with goat cheese before serving.

Serves 4

GREEK SALAD

3 tomatoes (Italian plum-type are good), cut in wedges
1 cucumber (fresh from the garden), sliced
1 red onion, thinly sliced
2 green peppers, cut in rings
6 tbsp. olive oil (Greek, if available)
2 tbsp. red wine vinegar
Salt and pepper to taste
$^1/_3$ lb. Feta cheese, crumbled (or cut into small squares)
2 dozen Kalamata olives (preferably pitted)
Crumbled, dried oregano

Place vegetables in large salad bowl.

Whisk together the olive oil, vinegar, salt, and pepper. Pour over the vegetables and toss gently. Top with Feta cheese and olives and sprinkle with oregano.

Serves 4

After a morning spent on "our" beach on Rhodes, Shirl and I would walk up to a little outdoor café where we enjoyed this salad for lunch. Use really good olive oil, preferably Greek, to enhance the fresh vegetables.
J.W. makes this salad in Cliff Hanger, *reissued as* Vineyard Fear.

—Phil

AVOCADO, SPINACH, CHIVE, AND PISTACHIO SALAD

1½ tsp. honey or Bavarian-style mustard
1 tbsp. Balsamic vinegar
2 tbsp. olive oil
Salt and freshly ground pepper
2 cups packed spinach leaves, torn into bite-sized pieces
1 ripe avocado, peeled, seeded, and diced
2 tbsp. chopped chives
2 tbsp. chopped pistachio nuts

Avocados are among the "super foods" as they are not only healthful but actually help the body absorb nutrients from other food. And . . . they are delish!

—Zee

In small bowl, whisk together first 4 ingredients (or use a good prepared honey mustard dressing, such as Vermont brand).

In salad bowl, combine next 3 ingredients and toss gently with dressing to mix. Sprinkle with pistachio nuts.

Note: Optional additions include crumbled, cooked bacon, and sliced mushrooms.

Serves 2

BROCCOLI/MACADAMIA NUT SALAD

$^{1}/_{2}$ cup mayonnaise

1 tbsp. granulated sugar

1 tbsp. cider vinegar

1 large head broccoli, washed, trimmed, and coarsely chopped

1 medium onion, finely chopped

1 cup Macadamia nuts, coarsely chopped

4 slices cooked bacon, crumbled

Whisk together first 3 ingredients. Add broccoli, onion, and nuts to dressing mixture. Mix until well coated. Refrigerate, covered, for at least 8 hours or overnight. Scatter crumbled bacon over top before serving.

Serves 4–6

Broccoli is another "super food" well known for its antioxidant qualities. It is also a favorite vegetable of the Jackson and Craig families, and who doesn't like macadamia nuts? (Did you know that before these nuts became popular with humans, Hawaiians used to feed them to their pigs? Lucky pigs!)

—Phil

COLD CARROT PENNY SALAD

2 lbs. carrots, peeled and sliced horizontally into thin discs
1 medium red onion, sliced thinly
1 sweet green pepper, diced
1 can tomato soup, undiluted
1 scant cup sugar
³/₄ cup vinegar
¹/₂ cup vegetable oil
1 tsp. prepared mustard
1 tsp. Worcestershire sauce
Salt and pepper to taste

Phil's mother introduced me to this recipe, and it's been a standby of ours for summer picnics since it doesn't suffer from lack of refrigeration. Any veggies that you would include in a typical marinated bean salad may be added for variety. I frequently add some drained and rinsed chick peas.

—Shirley

Cook carrots just until crisp tender, drain and cool. Layer carrots, onion, and pepper in a bowl. Mix remaining ingredients together and pour over vegetables. Refrigerate for 24 hours (or up to 3 weeks), stirring once or twice.

Optional additions would include beans (any variety), chick peas, artichoke hearts, ripe olives, etc.

BLACK BEAN AND RICE SALAD

2–3 cans of black beans, rinsed and drained

1 lb. frozen corn kernels, cooked (or 1 15-oz. can, drained)

2 cups long grain rice, cooked (or use rice pilaf, wild rice, or basmati rice)

1 large bell pepper, red or green, diced

1/2 cup red onion, chopped

1 tsp. salt

Dash of oregano

Optional ingredients:
Shredded Cheddar or Feta cheese

Sliced black olives

Marinated artichoke hearts

Dressing:
3/4 cup olive oil

1/4 cup balsamic vinegar

1 clove garlic, minced

1/4 tsp. salt

1 tsp. chili powder

1 tsp. oregano leaves

1/4 tsp. ground cumin

Dash of black pepper

Chopped fresh cilantro, to taste (or, if you can find it, Good Seasons Mexican Salad Dressing)

A great addition to a potluck get-together or a beach picnic. Shirl has never served this when someone didn't ask for the recipe. The recipe originally appeared at the back of A Shoot on Martha's Vineyard.

—Zee

Whisk dressing ingredients together and pour desired amount over bean salad. Sprinkle with chopped cilantro. Toss and serve.

Serves 6

MOLDED BEET AND CARROT SALAD

1 cup boiling beet juice (from canned beets or water in which you've cooked beets)
3-oz. pkg. lemon-flavored gelatin
$1/4$ lemon, peeled and seeded
1 tsp. salt
$1/4$ small onion, chopped
1 tbsp. prepared horseradish
2 carrots, cut in pieces
$1^1/2$ cups cooked beets, sliced

We tend to shy away from most gelatin salads, but this one makes a nice accompaniment to a roast beef dinner or to burgers done on the grill. It may, of course, be put into individual-serving sized molds, and it has the advantage of staying power when made ahead.

—Shirley

Add water to beet juice (if necessary) to make 1 cup. Put boiling juice and gelatin in blender, and run on low until gelatin is dissolved. Add lemon, salt, onion, and horseradish, and process on high until smooth. Add carrots, and run on low until chopped finely. Add beets, and run on low until chopped. Pour mixture into an oiled 1-qt. mold, and refrigerate until set.

Serve on salad greens with Ranch dressing.

Note: Salad may be made up to 5–6 days before serving.

Serves 6

POTATO (or Macaroni) SALAD

1 (16-oz.) box macaroni (elbows, shells, or spiral) or equal-volume amount of cooked and diced potatoes
$1/2$ large sweet green pepper, diced
$1/2$ large sweet red pepper, diced
1 cucumber, seeded and diced
2 stalks celery, thinly sliced
About 2 tbsp. red onion, finely diced
A few sliced radishes
Bacon bits
1 small can sliced ripe olives
3 sliced hard-boiled eggs
1 tsp. prepared mustard
Salt and pepper to taste
Mayonnaise
Italian dressing (if you are using potatoes)

If you use potatoes, drizzle a small amount of Italian dressing over them when they are hot.

Mix all ingredients, except hard-boiled egg slices, with mayonnaise to desired consistency. Gently fold in sliced eggs. Sprinkle with paprika before serving, and garnish with sprigs of parsley, if desired. Salt and pepper to taste.

Serves 4–6

Everyone has a potato salad recipe. This one is the Craig family favorite. If you don't like potatoes or you've run out of potatoes, you can use macaroni. I have eaten a lot of potato salads, but never one better than this.

—Phil

SALAD ORIENTAL

Try this as an accompaniment to an Asian menu.

—J.W.

Arrange:
Cooked shrimp,
Avocado slices,
Hard-cooked egg slices, and
Chow mein noodles on
Boston-type lettuce leaves.
Dress with Thousand Island dressing.

AZTEC SALAD

As you can see from the ingredients, this salad has a Mexican air. It works well as a luncheon dish, served with triangles of toasted pita bread or as an accompaniment to a south-of-the-border entrée.

—J.W.

4 ripe avocados, peeled, halved, and seeded
1¹/₂ cups drained whole kernel corn (12-oz. can)
1 cup kidney beans, drained and rinsed
¹/₂ cup onion, chopped
¹/₃ cup green pepper, chopped (may use mixture of sweet and chili peppers)
2 tbsp. chopped pimiento or roasted red peppers

Fill avocado halves with mixture of next 5 ingredients, moistened with:

¹/₂ cup Catalina French Dressing

Serves 8

HONEY-MUSTARD DRESSING

$^1/_3$ cup vegetable oil
2 tbsp. cider vinegar
1 tbsp. Dijon mustard
1 tbsp. honey
$^1/_4$ tsp. each of salt and pepper

Whisk ingredients until well blended. Refrigerate and shake well before serving.

You can buy excellent honey-mustard dressing in your grocery store, but if you feel like making your own, here's a good recipe.

—Zee

GARLIC CROUTONS

French bread (a piece about the size of a sub roll) cut with serrated knife into 1″ cubes
$^1/_4$ cup unsalted butter
1 large clove garlic, minced

Preheat oven to 375°. Place butter and garlic in glass bowl. Microwave for 1 minute.

You can buy croutons, but these are better.

—J.W.

Pour garlic butter over bread cubes and toss to coat evenly.

Spread cubes in single layer in baking pan. Bake 10–15 minutes, stirring once or twice, until golden. Cool before storing in airtight container.

ORIENTAL COLE SLAW

$^1/_2$ pkg. cole slaw or broccoli slaw mix (up to 8 cups)
$^3/_4$ cup chopped green onion (or $^1/_2$ cup diced red onion)
1 pkg. Ramen oriental-flavored noodles, not cooked
$^1/_2$ cup slivered almonds (or may use part sunflower seeds)
2 tbsp. sesame seeds
3 tbsp. white wine vinegar or rice wine vinegar
2 tbsp. sugar
$^1/_2$ cup, or less, canola oil

This is a refreshing variation on conventional cole slaw. The secret ingredient is the Ramen oriental-flavored noodles. Give it a try. You'll keep on using the recipe.

—Zee

Dissolve 2 tbsp. sugar with 3 tbsp. vinegar. Add $^1/_2$ cup oil and the flavor packet from the Ramen noodles. Whisk together until well blended. Set this dressing aside.

Toast $^1/_2$ cup slivered almonds with 2 tbsp. sesame seeds at 350° for about 5 minutes. (Watch carefully.)

Toss dressing with slaw mix and refrigerate. Drain excess dressing, and toss slaw with almond mixture and broken Ramen noodles $^1/_2$ hour before serving.

PEAR/GORGONZOLA SALAD
WITH TOASTED WALNUTS

All of the amounts in this recipe are flexible, depending
upon your taste and how many you want to serve. The
basic ingredients include:

Mesclun greens
Anjou pears
Gorgonzola cheese (crumbled)
Balsamic vinaigrette
Walnut pieces (toasted)

In a large salad plate, lay down a good layer of mesclun
greens. Halve each pear, remove core, and cut wedges into
thin slivers (best done on a mandoline). Fan sliced pears on
top of greens. Crumble cheese over all, dress with a small
amount of balsamic vinaigrette, and sprinkle each serving
with walnut pieces.

*Shirley enjoyed this salad
at a local restaurant and
came up with this version
to serve at home, where
she takes some care
arranging the pear
slices for an attractive
presentation. I think
it's terrific!*

—Phil

FRENCH LENTIL SALAD

2 cups French lentils

1 tsp. salt

10 sprigs Italian parsley

15 sprigs sweet basil

4 cloves garlic (unpeeled and slightly crushed)

1 carrot (peeled and finely diced)

1 rib celery (finely diced)

1 red onion (peeled and finely diced), about 1 cup

$^1/_3$ cup olive oil

1 or 2 large portobello mushroom caps (chopped and sautéed)

8 oz. chickpeas (drained and rinsed)

1 cup cooked wild and long grain rice or Basmati rice (may use leftover rice)

3 plum tomatoes (seeded and chopped)

8 oz. Feta cheese (crumbled)

Salt and pepper to taste

Toasted piñon nuts

Sliced ripe olives (or Kalamata olives)

Balsamic vinaigrette

So the recipe is long, but it's worth every bit of effort you put into making it. Both Zee and I tend toward vegetarian fare, but even Phil and J.W. enjoy this concoction. The recipe may be made ahead (and even frozen) before adding the vinaigrette, tomatoes, nuts, cheese, and basil garnish.

—Shirley

Rinse lentils, put in saucepan, and barely cover with cold water (about 5 cups). Add 1 tsp. salt.

Make a bouquet garni using some of the parsley, some of the basil, and 4 cloves garlic tied up in a piece of cheesecloth, and add to saucepan. Bring lentils to a boil, then reduce heat and simmer, uncovered, for 10 minutes (do not overcook).

Add carrot, celery, and onions to lentils and simmer for an additional 10–15 minutes, until lentils are tender but al dente. Add more hot water, $^1/_4$ cup at a time, while simmering, if needed. Very little, if any, water should remain in pan when lentils are done. Drain off any remaining water before proceeding.

Discard bouquet garni, and toss lentil mixture with ¹/₃ cup of olive oil. Spread lentil mixture on rimmed baking sheets and cool to room temperature. When cool, transfer to large bowl and mix with sautéed mushroom pieces, chickpeas, and cooked rice. Add a little more olive oil if mixture seems too dry, and adjust seasonings if necessary. May be frozen at this point.

Dress with a small amount of your favorite balsamic vinaigrette (made with olive oil and a bit of minced garlic) and refrigerate, covered, for at least an hour.

When ready to serve, mix in chopped tomatoes and some sliced olives. After salad is plated, sprinkle with toasted piñon nuts, some Feta cheese, and some of the remaining basil leaves, cut into fine strips. Pass extra vinaigrette if desired.

"Red onions are especially divine.
I hold a slice up to the sunlight pouring in
through the kitchen window, and it glows
like a fine piece of antique glass."
—MARY HAYES GRIECO, *THE KITCHEN MYSTIC*

SESAME NOODLES

1 pkg. linguini or soft Chinese noodles (cooked and drained)

7 tbsp. soy sauce

1 tbsp. hot pepper oil

4 tbsp. balsamic vinegar

$\frac{1}{2}$ tsp. salt

1–2 tbsp. sugar

1 tbsp. fresh ginger, grated

1 tbsp. minced garlic

1 cup snow peas, blanched briefly and refreshed under cold water

2 tbsp. sesame seeds, briefly toasted

Poached chicken chunks or cooked shrimp (optional)

This salad is a good change of pace from more usual ones.

—Shirley

Mix all ingredients (except noodles, peas, and sesame seeds) together for sauce. Pour over noodles and chill. Just before serving, add peas and toasted sesame seeds. You may add poached chicken chunks or cooked shrimp if desired.

This dish should be served well chilled, so try to make it at least several hours before serving. Double the recipe to feed a crowd.

Entrées

"ZEE HAD THE LAST OF THE SCALLOPS
IN THE FRIDGE AND WAS WORKING ON
SUPPER. SCALLOPS, OF COURSE. HER
PLAN, I SAW, WAS TO FRY THEM UP WITH
GARLIC BUTTER AND SERVE THEM OVER
RICE WITH BROCCOLI ON THE SIDE.
A WINNING MEAL, FOR SURE."

—J.W., IN *VINEYARD PREY*

STUFFED BLUEFISH

1 medium (6- to 8-lb.) bluefish (cleaned whole fish or filleted)
Herbed stuffing mix—enough to fill fish cavity or sandwich between fillets
Italian salad dressing
Lemon wedges

Bluefish generally arrive in Martha's Vineyard waters about the second week in May, as they come up from the Carolinas on their way to Nova Scotia and points north. Vineyard fishermen usually get the first ones from boats, but then the fish come close to shore and J.W. and Zee are waiting for them at Wasque. J.W. cooks this recipe in A Beautiful Place to Die *and* A Case of Vineyard Poison. We first printed the recipe in *A Deadly Vineyard Holiday.*

—Phil

Place fish in baking pan which has been lined with greased foil. Mix stuffing according to package directions, or make your own. Fill cavity of fish with stuffing, or put stuffing between fillets. Drizzle salad dressing over fish. Bake in preheated 400° oven for about 20 minutes or until fish flakes easily. Remove fish to heated platter and garnish with lemon wedges.

Serves 6–8

BROILED BLUEFISH WITH MUSTARD, LEMON, AND DILL SAUCE

1½ lbs. fresh bluefish fillets, cut into serving-size portions
1–2 tbsp. olive oil
1 tbsp. butter
⅓ cup milk
3 tbsp. Dijon mustard
1 tbsp. fresh dill, chopped
Salt and pepper to taste
½ tsp. fresh lemon juice (or to taste)

Brush bluefish with olive oil. Place in shallow, greased pan and place 3″ from heat in preheated broiler. For ½″-thick pieces, broil for about 5 minutes (about 8–10 minutes for 1″-thick pieces).

While fish is cooking, combine butter with milk in a small saucepan. Heat until butter has melted. Stir in mustard, dill, salt, pepper, and lemon juice. Reheat and serve over fish pieces.

Serves 4

Early in the season, when the bluefish are fighting for the privilege of biting your lure, you sometimes bring home more than you can eat, so you give them away to friends or elderly people who can no longer go out and catch their own. Then you bring yours home and ponder new ways to cook them. This is one of those ways. J.W. cooks this in Death on a Vineyard Beach.

—Shirley

GRILLED STRIPED BASS WITH MUSTARD, MAYO, AND DILL SAUCE

2-lb. fillet of striped bass
$^1/_4$ cup mayonnaise
$^1/_4$ cup Dijon mustard
1 tbsp. finely chopped dill
$1^1/_2$ tsp. lime juice
$1^1/_2$ tsp. brown sugar
Salt and pepper to taste
Vegetable oil

Striped bass is a favorite Atlantic game fish. The annual Martha's Vineyard Bass and Bluefish Derby draws hundreds of entries every fall, and J.W. and Zee are two of them. Much to J.W.'s chagrin, he has never caught a 40-pound bass, although Zee has caught more than one. This recipe is very simple and very satisfying. A mustard, mayo, and dill sauce goes very well with a number of different fish, including bluefish, bass, sole, and mackerel.

—Phil

In a bowl, mix a sauce of mayonnaise, mustard, dill, lime juice, brown sugar, and a bit of pepper.

Rub skin-side of the bass fillet with oil, and sprinkle with salt and pepper. Place on grill, skin-side down.

Spread sauce on top of fillet. Close grill, and cook over moderate heat until fish is flaky (about 25 minutes).

Serve hot or at room temperature.

Makes an excellent sandwich filling!

SOLE WITH MUSTARD, MAYO, AND DILL SAUCE

4 sole fillets (1½–2 lb. total)
½ cup mayonnaise
2 tbsp. Dijon-style mustard
Fresh dill, snipped

Preheat oven to 400°. Place fillets in single layer in buttered shallow baking pan. Mix mayonnaise and mustard together and spread over fillets. Sprinkle with snipped dill. Bake at 400° about 15 minutes or until fish flakes easily.

The meat of flounder, sole, or fluke—members of the same flat fish family—is delicate and white and can be overpowered by too strong a sauce.

—Shirley

BROILED SPANISH MACKEREL

Fillet Spanish mackerel.

Smear fillet with a mixture of mayonnaise mixed with a little Dijonaise mustard.

Sprinkle fillets with some fresh, or dried, dill weed.

Broil, in preheated broiler, until fish flakes (time depends on thickness of fillets).

Serve with lemon wedges.

Serves 4

Spanish mackerel isn't sold in too many places because it's not caught nearly as often as other game fish such as bluefish and bass. When J.W. and Zee catch some, they take them all home to feed the Jacksons. J.W. cooks this in The Double-Minded Men, *which was later retitled* Vineyard Deceit.

—Shirley

BLUEFISH WITH MUSTARD/HORSERADISH SAUCE

2 lbs. bluefish fillets
$^1/_4$ cup mayonnaise
$^1/_4$ cup Dijon style mustard
1 tsp. prepared horseradish

*Many fish dishes are
very simple. This is one
of them. It uses a sauce
that might be a little
overpowering on the
meat of a more delicate
fish, but is just right for
the strong-flavored
bluefish. The recipe was
printed in* Second Sight.

—Zee

Place fillets skin side down on greased foil in baking pan.
Mix remaining ingredients together and spread on fillets.
Bake in preheated 400° oven for about 20 minutes or until
fish is opaque and flakes easily. Remove fish to heated platter.
Garnish with dill sprigs if desired.

Fish may also be cooked in broiler. Place about 4″ from
broiler unit and broil 7–10 minutes (depending on thickness
of fillets) or until fish is done.

Serves 4

FRIED STRIPED BASS

*This is another good,
simple way to cook
striped bass. If you like
fish and chips, you'll like
this dish.*

—Zee

Cut bass fillet into 2-in. squares. Beat an egg. Coat the
squares in the beaten egg, then shake them in a bag of
Bisquick. Heat a small amount of olive oil in a frying pan,
and fry 3 or 4 minutes on a side, turning once. Take them
out when you think they're done. Serve with tartar sauce.

GRILLED STRIPED BASS WITH HERB BUTTER

2- to 3-lb. striped bass fillet
Herb butter
Salt and pepper to taste

To make herb butter, combine:
$1/2$ cup butter or margarine
2 tbsp. minced fresh parsley
2 tbsp. minced fresh basil
1 tbsp. minced fresh thyme
$1/4$ tsp. ground pepper
Makes about $3/4$ cup

Sprinkle bass with salt and pepper, and place on well-greased grill at medium heat. Cover with herb butter mixture, and cook under closed grill or aluminum foil tent, basting frequently with remaining herb butter mixture, for 10–15 minutes per inch thickness of fish or until fish is flaky. Serve with remaining herb-butter sauce, if there is any.

Serves 6–8

Striped bass and bluefish seem to thrive in opposite cycles. When the bass are rare, the bluefish are plentiful, and vice versa. No one really knows why. As we write this, the bass are increasing in population and the blues are becoming harder to catch. Sometime in the future the opposite may be true.

—Shirley

BRADY'S BAKED STRIPED BASS

Brady Coyne, the protagonist in a series of mystery novels by William G. Tapply, practices law to support his fly-casting habit. Brady and J.W. have appeared together in three novels. Brady is a good cook of wild game of all kinds—fish, fowl, and mammal. This is his take on striped bass. Unlike Zee, who prefers flounder, Brady considers freshly caught striped bass the best eating fish from the sea. This recipe appears in the back of Second Sight.

—Phil

You need a fresh bass fillet. Brush both sides of the fillet with olive oil and lay in a shallow baking dish. Sprinkle the fillet with crushed Ritz cracker crumbs. Cover with very thin lemon slices. Dot generously with hunks of butter. Add salt and fresh-ground pepper. Bake in a preheated 375° oven for 25 minutes. Serve with a robust white wine, a fresh seasonal green vegetable, and boiled baby red potatoes sprinkled with parsley. Delish!

FALSE ALBACORE

1 false albacore (if you can catch one), bled well immediately
after catching, filleted and skinned
$1/2$ cup lemon juice
$1/4$ cup olive oil
1 tsp. salt
1 tsp. dried oregano leaves
2 cloves minced garlic
$1/2$ tsp. pepper

Mix all ingredients (except fish) together and place in
nonreactive bowl or plastic bag. Cut fish fillets into
chunks and put into marinade mixture. Marinate
overnight in refrigerator.

Remove fish from marinade, and grill just until it is opaque
and flakes easily. Serve with lemon slices or tartar sauce.

Number served depends on size of fish and the biases
of diners.

*Yes, Virginia, you can
eat false albacore. It is
one of the four prize fish
in the famous Martha's
Vineyard Bass and
Bluefish Derby. (The
others are bonito and, of
course, striped bass and
bluefish.) Shirl wants
false albacore removed
from the prize list because
most fishermen don't eat
the fish, believing it's not
good tasting. Shirl, like
many people, disapproves
of killing animals you
don't eat. But false
albacore remains in the
Derby, so Shirl offers
this recipe as evidence
that the fish is actually
very tasty, in the hope
that fishermen will
begin eating their catch
instead of throwing it
away after the weigh-in.*
—Phil

ROLLED FILLET OF SOLE

6 fillets of sole (or any whitefish)—about 2 lbs.
1/4 cup plus 2 tbsp. olive oil
2 tbsp. lemon juice
1 medium clove garlic, minced
2 tbsp. chopped chives
1 tsp. seasoned salt
1/2 cup chopped mushrooms
1/4 cup pine nuts
2 cups chopped fresh spinach
1/4 cup sliced scallions
Dash of Mongolian Fire oil or hot sauce
Watercress sprigs (optional)
Lemon slices

Zee loves flounder and cooks it in several ways. This one is a bit fancier than most, because it includes such delicacies as mushrooms and pine nuts, and requires rolling.

—J.W.

Wash fish, pat dry, and arrange in buttered shallow baking dish.

Combine 1/4 cup olive oil, Mongolian Fire oil, lemon juice, garlic, chives, and seasoned salt, and pour over fish to coat well. Cover and refrigerate several hours, turning occasionally.

Brown mushrooms and nuts in skillet in remaining olive oil. Add spinach and scallions. Sauté several minutes to soften spinach, stirring frequently.

Preheat oven to 400°. Remove fish from marinade. Divide filling among fillets, roll up and arrange, seam side down, in baking dish. Spoon marinade over fish. Bake 15 minutes or until fish flakes easily. Garnish with lemon slices and watercress.

Serves 6

FISH FILLETS FLORENTINE

4 fillets of mild-flavored whitefish, such as flounder or sole
(about 5 oz. each)
1 (10-oz.) box frozen, chopped spinach, cooked according to
package directions, cooled and squeezed dry
¼ cup mayonnaise
2 tsp. lemon juice
1 tbsp. Dijon mustard
¾ tsp. garlic powder
½ tsp. salt
¼ tsp. pepper
2 drops hot-pepper sauce (or to taste)
2 tbsp. butter or oleo
1 tsp. paprika
¼ cup toasted piñon nuts

*Another rolled fish
dish, this one with an
Italian flair.*

—J.W.

Heat oven to 375°.

Mix spinach, mayonnaise, lemon juice, mustard, garlic powder, salt, pepper, hot sauce and piñon nuts until blended. Spoon ¼ cup mixture onto wide end of each fillet. Roll up fillets and place, seam sides down, in buttered 8″-square baking dish. Dot with butter and sprinkle with paprika. Bake 12–15 minutes or until fish is opaque in middle.

Serves 4

FLOUNDER ALMANDINE

1½–2 lbs. flounder fillets (or other mild whitefish)
½ cup flour
½ tsp. paprika
¼ tsp. salt
¼ tsp. pepper
4–6 tbsp. unsalted butter
½ cup sliced almonds

This is a lovely way to eat flounder. It's very simple to prepare but tastes like it took you all day.

—Shirley

Mix flour, paprika, salt, and pepper together. Dry fillets well and dredge in flour mixture, shaking off excess. Melt butter in skillet over medium-high heat. Sauté fish (about 2 minutes per side) in hot butter. Reduce heat and cook just until fish is opaque. Remove fish. Add more butter to skillet if necessary; add almonds and cook just until golden. Pour almonds over fish and serve immediately.

Serves 4

SCANDINAVIAN FISHBAKE

1 lb. cod or other whitefish
10 small onions
4 tbsp. butter
2¹/₂ tbsp. flour
³/₄ cup milk
¹/₂ cup water
2 chicken bouillon cubes
Salt
White pepper
¹/₂ cup light cream
¹/₄ cup grated Parmesan cheese
Dill for garnish

This dish is incredibly simple to make and incredibly good to eat. You can use any whitefish you like, and you'll end up with a dish that makes your taste buds jump up and down with joy. This recipe appears in the back of Vineyard Blues.

—Phil

Peel and slice onions. Place in small skillet, add 2 tbsp. water and simmer covered, until onions are soft and transparent. Remove cover and add 2 tbsp. butter. Cook until water evaporates. Place onions on bottom of an ovenproof dish, and cover with skinless fish fillets. Salt lightly and set aside.

Melt remaining 2 tbsp. butter and add flour, stirring until smooth. Add remaining ingredients (except cheese) and stir constantly over medium heat until thickened. Pour sauce over fish and cover with grated cheese. Bake at 350° for 25–30 minutes. Garnish with chopped dill and serve with rice or boiled potatoes.

Serves 4

SEAFOOD CASSEROLE

½ green pepper, chopped
¼ cup onion, chopped
½ lb. sliced mushrooms

A simple, elegant dish requiring little preparation. You can make it the day before you eat it, if you wish. J.W. cooks this casserole in A Vineyard Killing, *and the recipe may be found at the back of that book.*

—Zee

Sauté these ingredients in 3–4 tbsp. butter, then add:
1 can cream of mushroom soup
8 oz. sour cream
3 cups cooked rice
1 lb. precooked seafood (any combination of crabmeat, shrimp, lobster, scallops, or flaked whitefish)

Mix well, season with celery salt and pepper, and place in baking dish.

Top with buttered crumbs and some bacon bits (and, if you wish, green or red pepper rings, red pepper, or pimiento).

Bake at 300° for 30 minutes or until hot, and serve immediately.

Serves 4

LOBSTER CASSEROLE

6 tbsp. butter
6 tbsp. flour
3 lbs. cooked fresh lobster meat, cut in chunks
3 tbsp. grated Parmesan cheese
3 cups light cream or milk (add more if needed)
Marsala wine to taste
2^1/$_2$ cups fresh bread crumbs
2 tbsp. butter

Make a roux of butter and flour; stir and cook for 5 minutes. Add lobster meat and Parmesan cheese, and stir over low heat. Heat cream or milk and add. Stir constantly. Let sauce cook but not boil. Add more milk if necessary. Add Marsala wine to taste. Set mixture aside.

Put bread crumbs, dotted with butter, on cookie sheet. Place in 325° oven. After butter melts and crumbs are lightly toasted, stir with fork and remove from oven. Turn off oven. Put lobster mixture in casserole, and cover with toasted bread crumbs.

Let cool before placing in fridge, cover with plastic wrap. To reheat and serve, place in 325° oven for 20 minutes or until sauce is hot and bubbly.

Serve with rice and crusty bread.

Serves 8

When lobsters are on sale, invite your best friends to dinner and serve this special casserole. Delish indeed!
—J.W.

AT-HOME "CLAMBAKE"

Soft-shelled steamer clams (1–2 qts. per serving)
New potatoes
Small to medium onions
Fresh sweet corn
Kielbasa or linguisa (cut into 3″ lengths)

A New England clambake can be concocted at the beach or indoors or almost anywhere else. For most people, the "At-Home Clambake" is the easiest. The clams and all other ingredients are actually steamed rather than baked, but the result is very much like that achieved when the same ingredients are cooked over rockweed in a pit at the beach. J.W. creates clambakes in A Case of Vineyard Poison.

—Phil

In a large steaming kettle, place a 6″ layer of rockweed, if available (not absolutely necessary). Add a couple of inches of water. Prick the washed potatoes with a fork and arrange on top of the rockweed. Add the onions. Cover potatoes and onions with a little more rockweed. When water boils, lower heat, cover steamer, and steam for about 30 minutes. Add de-sanded clams (see note), sweet corn, and kielbasa or linguisa.

Top with a little more rockweed and steam until clams open (about 10–15 minutes). All cooking times are approximate and depend upon the size of the vegetables and the amounts in the steamer kettle. The ingredients in the kettle may be separated by layers of cheesecloth or by putting them in separate cheesecloth bags, to facilitate serving, if desired. All ingredients can be cooked in separate pots, if it seems easier to test for doneness that way, and combined at the end.

The clams should be served with cups of strained broth (from the steamer pot), so that they may be rinsed of any remaining sand, and cups of melted butter for dipping.

Note: Clams can be de-sanded by soaking them overnight in saltwater (preferably ocean water). Keep the soaking clams in a cool spot. They will disgorge the sand from their little bellies.

Other ingredients, such as lobsters, crabs, mussels, etc., may be added to your clambake. If you are not using rockweed in the bottom of your steamer pot, put all of the ingredients in the top section of the steamer so that they will not be resting directly in the water. Clams will become tough if overcooked. They are done when their shells open.

FRIED CLAMS WITH TARTAR SAUCE

Dip shucked clams in evaporated milk.

Dredge clams in a mixture of 1 part pastry flour to 3 parts yellow cornmeal (may add a dash of cayenne pepper or Cajun seafood seasoning to mix). Shake off excess.

Heat lard (or combination of lard and vegetable oil) in fryer to 350° and fry clams (a few at a time to prevent lowering temperature of fat) for about 1 minute.

Drain on absorbent paper and keep warm until all clams are fried.

For Tartar Sauce, see page 173.

Heaven on earth. Phil loves fried clams, fried onion rings, fried scallops, and fried almost anything else. I think his absolutely favorite meal would be fried salt, if he could get it. J.W. fries clams in The Double-Minded Men, *reissued as* Vineyard Deceit.

—Shirley

SCALLOPS ST. JACQUE

2½ lbs. bay scallops (or sea scallops cut in two)
½ lb. mushrooms (sliced)
10 tbsp. butter
½ cup dry white wine
1 minced onion
1 bay leaf
1 tsp. dried thyme
Juice of ½ lemon
4 tsp. flour
4 egg yolks, beaten
2 cups heavy cream or milk*
¼ cup freshly grated Parmesan cheese
4 tbsp. bread crumbs

Scallops are the classic ingredient in this excellent dish, but it can also be made with other shellfish or white fin fish. If you don't have scallops, try it with flounder or hake, etc. J.W. has never cooked it with salmon or trout but suspects it would be delish using either. The recipe may be found at the back of First Light.

—Phil

Bring to boil: mushrooms, 4 tbsp. butter, white wine, minced onion, bay leaf, thyme, and lemon juice. Simmer 3 minutes. Add scallops and simmer 2 minutes more. Set aside.

To make roux: first, melt second 4 tbsp. butter. Slowly whisk in flour and stir until mixture bubbles (do not brown). Gradually whisk in 1 cup of cream (or milk) until mixture is smooth.

Next, drain scallops and reserve fluid. Add fluid to above mixture, whisking over medium heat until thickened. Add 1 tsp. salt and ½ tsp. pepper (white pepper if you have it).

Next, to beaten egg yolks add the second cup of cream (or milk). Stir. Whisk a little of the egg mixture into above sauce, then whisk in remaining egg mixture. Bring sauce just to a boil, but not boiling. This roux should coat a metal spoon.

Place scallops in lightly greased casserole dish. Remove bay leaf, and spoon roux over fish. Combine Parmesan cheese and bread crumbs, and spread over scallops. Drizzle with last 2 tbsp. melted butter. Casserole may be cooled then covered and refrigerated at this point.

Before baking, return casserole to room temperature and bake, uncovered, in preheated 350° oven for 25 minutes or until just heated through. Brown top under broiler just before serving. Serve over rice.

Makes 6–8 servings

* Skim milk works fine in this recipe, and the end result tastes far more caloric than it actually is.

RITZ SCALLOPS

Preheat oven to 375°.

1 lb. bay scallops
¼ to ½ cup melted butter
1 cup crushed Ritz cracker crumbs

Layer cracker crumbs and scallops in greased casserole dish. Pour melted butter over all. Bake at 375° for 25 minutes.

Serves 4

This recipe is so simple and so unfailingly delicious. If you don't happen to have any scallops, try using shrimp or flounder. The recipe was also published in A Deadly Vineyard Holiday.

—Shirley

STIR-FRIED SCALLOPS AND VEGETABLES

½ lb. bay scallops
2 tbsp. soy sauce
1 tbsp. dry sherry (or 1 tsp. lemon juice)
1 clove garlic, minced
¼ tsp. ground ginger
2 tbsp. peanut oil
2 ribs celery, thinly sliced on diagonal
2 green onions, with tops, cut in 1″ pieces
1 (10-oz.) pkg. frozen tiny peas (thawed and well drained),
or snowpeas
⅓ cup sliced radishes
Hot cooked rice

Scallops are sweet and tender and require very little cooking. J.W. and Phil like to eat them raw, in fact. In this recipe they're part of a one-dish meal prepared in a skillet or wok. As is the case with most of the recipes in this book, you can vary the ingredients to suit your own taste. J.W. cooks this in A Case of Vineyard Poison *and* Cliff Hanger, *reissued as* Vineyard Fear.

—Shirley

Place scallops in mixing bowl with soy sauce, sherry, garlic, and ginger. Toss gently and marinate while preparing other ingredients.

In skillet or wok, heat oil until very hot. Add celery and onions and stir-fry to crisp tender, about 2 minutes. Push to side of skillet and add scallops with marinade. Cook until fork tender (1 to 2 minutes). Add peas and heat through. Toss to mix. Sprinkle with radishes. Serve over rice with additional soy sauce.

Serves 4

SCALLOPS IN SHERRY-MUSTARD SAUCE

1 lb. bay scallops
1 tsp. extra virgin olive oil
4 tbsp. fresh thyme, chopped
Juice of 1 lemon
2 tbsp. dry sherry
1 tbsp. Dijon-style mustard
Italian parsley

Marinate scallops in mixture of thyme and lemon juice for 15–20 minutes. Heat oil in skillet and sauté scallops for about 1 minute. Remove scallops to warm plate. Add sherry, mustard, and reserved marinade to skillet. Bring to a boil. Reduce slightly and pour over scallops. Sprinkle with chopped parsley.

Scallops may be served over rice or linguini.

Serves 6

A little sherry does wonders for many dishes. In this recipe it turns a simply prepared entrée into something special. This recipe appears in the back of Vineyard Prey.

—J.W.

SCALLOPS IN WINE

2 lbs. scallops
1¹/₄ cup dry white wine
³/₄ tsp. salt
¹/₈ tsp. pepper
1 bay leaf
1 celery stalk (with leaves)
¹/₂ cup butter
¹/₂ lb. fresh mushrooms, sliced
¹/₄ cup chopped green onion
¹/₄ cup chopped green bell pepper
¹/₄ cup flour
2 egg yolks
¹/₄ cup heavy cream
¹/₄ tsp. dried thyme leaves
2 tbsp. chopped pimiento
¹/₄ cup grated Parmesan cheese
¹/₄ cup buttered bread crumbs

This dish can also be served for an elegant lunch accompanied by a salad such as Orange/Avocado/Red Onion Salad (see page 69). This recipe appears in the back of Vineyard Prey.

—Shirley

In medium saucepan, combine scallops, wine, salt, pepper, bay leaf, celery, thyme, pimiento, and ³/₄ cup water. Bring to boil, reduce heat and simmer, covered, for about 5 minutes. Drain scallops, reserving liquid. Discard bay leaf and celery.

In 4 tbsp. butter, sauté mushrooms 2 minutes. Add onion and green pepper, and sauté 5 minutes more. Set aside.

Melt the rest of the butter, remove from heat, and stir in flour until smooth.

Gradually stir in reserved liquid from scallops. Bring to boiling point, stirring constantly, reduce heat, and simmer 1 minute.

In small bowl, mix egg yolks lightly with cream. Stir in some of hot mixture, then add egg mixture to sauce. Cook, stirring, over low heat, about 5 minutes or until thickened.

Combine all ingredients; pour into individual baking shells or into baking dish. Top with buttered crumbs and Parmesan cheese. Bake at 400° for 15 minutes or until browned and bubbly.

Serves 8

SCALLOPS TIKKA

1 lb. bay scallops
Mix together about 4 tbsp. each of:
Tikka paste (available in Indian ethnic food section)
Sour cream or plain yogurt (amounts may be varied to your liking)

Gently stir scallops into mixture. Remove scallops and spread in single layer in greased oven-proof pan. Sprinkle with buttered bread or cracker crumbs seasoned with a small amount of Cajun seafood seasoning.

Broil 3–4 inches from heat for about 5 minutes.

Serves 4

If you like Indian food, this dish will give you joy. It's Shirley's creation, because as far as we know there are no scallops in Indian waters. The recipe appears in the back of Vineyard Prey.

—Phil

OYSTERS ROCKEFELLER

Preheat oven to 475°.

36 medium-sized oysters on the half shell
Creamed Spinach (see page 155)

Half fill oyster shell with creamed spinach. Top each with:

Ever wonder what brave soul first ate an oyster? Most people who shy away from raw oysters will relish this dish. Off-season is the best time to prepare it, though some Vineyard oysters are harvested from the deep ponds even in summer. J.W. cooks this in A Beautiful Place to Die *and* Off Season.

—Phil

1 shucked oyster
$^1/_2$–1 tsp. chopped fresh parsley
A few drops of lemon juice and Worcestershire sauce
A 1″-square piece of partially cooked bacon

Embed the stuffed shell in pans of rock salt (to steady them and protect them from too much heat) and bake at 475° for about 10 minutes or until plump. Run briefly under broiler to brown. Serve immediately.

Serves 6

JESSICA'S CAJUN SEAFOOD WITH FETTUCCINE

1½ pounds shrimp (peeled and deveined) or ¾ lb. each of
shrimp and bay scallops
1 tbsp. olive oil
1 tbsp. Cajun seasoning
12 oz. fettuccine pasta
1 tbsp. unsalted butter
3 cups mushrooms, sliced
1 tbsp. shallots, chopped
⅔ cup chicken broth
½ cup dairy sour cream
1 tbsp. cornstarch
1 cup chicken broth
1 (7 oz.) jar roasted sweet red peppers
1 tbsp. capers, drained

*My granddaughter
Jessica has recently
developed an interest in
cooking things other
than dessert. She tried
this out on her family
and friends, and says
they approved.*

—Shirley

Mix seafood, oil, and Cajun seasoning in a bowl. Set aside.

Cook fettuccine according to directions on the package,
until al dente.

In a large frying pan, melt butter over medium heat. Sauté
mushrooms and shallots in butter until tender. Remove from
pan, add seafood, and cook until shrimp are pink-about 2-3
minutes (bay scallops take about the same amount of cooking time). Remove seafood from pan. Add the ⅔ cup chicken
broth to pan, bring to a boil and cook, uncovered, until
broth is reduced to ¼ cup (about 3 minutes).

In a small bowl, combine sour cream, cornstarch, and the
cup of chicken broth. Whisk until smooth. Stir into reduced
chicken broth in frying pan and cook, stirring, until it
becomes thick and bubbly.

Cook for 1 more minute. Stir in seafood and mushroom
mixture, and then add roasted red peppers and capers. Heat
through. Season as desired. Serve over fettuccine.

Serves 4-6

BAKED SHRIMP WITH SHERRY AND GARLIC

1¹/₂ lbs. large shrimp (shelled, deveined and patted dry)
¹/₄ cup olive oil
3 tbsp. dry sherry
3 large cloves garlic
¹/₂ tsp. crushed thyme leaves
¹/₄ tsp. salt
¹/₈ tsp. crushed red pepper
Lemon wedges

J.W. cooks a variation of this, using flounder instead of shrimp, in A Shoot on Martha's Vineyard. *You can also use scallops or a mixture of scallops and shrimp. Whatever fish or shellfish is used, the guests in the Jackson household love it. The amazingly simple recipe may be found at the back of* A Shoot on Martha's Vineyard.

—Zee

Arrange shrimp, slightly apart in single layer, in greased, shallow baking dish. Mix remaining ingredients and pour over shrimp. Bake in preheated 400° oven, turning once, 8 minutes or until shrimps are pink and barely opaque throughout. Serve over rice with pan juices.

A citrus salad, such as Orange/Avocado/Red Onion Salad (see page 69), goes well with this.

Serves 4

SHRIMP WITH SNOW PEAS

Cooking sauce:

1 tsp. cornstarch
1/4 tsp. ground ginger
2 tbsp. soy sauce
2 tbsp. dry sherry
1/2 cup chicken broth

Stir all ingredients until well mixed and set aside.

3 tbsp. peanut oil
1 clove garlic, minced
1 lb. medium raw shrimp, shelled and deveined
1 1/2 cups snow peas, ends and strings removed (or 6-oz. package of frozen pea pods, thawed)
1 (8-oz.) can sliced water chestnuts
3 scallions, thinly sliced, including tops

Place wok over high heat. When wok is hot, add oil and heat until hot. Add garlic and shrimp, and stir-fry for about a minute. Add pea pods and stir-fry for about 3 minutes (30 seconds if using thawed, frozen pea pods).

Add water chestnuts and scallions, and stir to mix. Stir in cooking sauce, and continue to stir until sauce boils and thickens and shrimp turn pink. Serve over rice or noodles.

Serves 4

Try this recipe when the edible snow-pea vines are producing more of their delicious pods than you can eat while picking. Bonus: You won't spend much time in the kitchen preparing this.

—Shirley

QUICK COQ AU VIN

It doesn't get any easier or tastier than this—a great make-ahead dish that will keep for less-than-prompt dinner guests. You can add mushrooms and substitute chicken bouillon for beef bouillon if you like. The recipe first appeared at the back of Vineyard Shadows.

—Zee

2 whole chicken breasts, split, skinned and boned (or up to 8 pieces of chicken parts)
1½ cups dry red wine
1 (1⅜ oz.) pkg. dry onion soup mix
1 beef bouillon cube

Place all ingredients in a 2-qt. casserole dish. Cover and bake at 350° for 2 hours. Serve over rice or riced potatoes.

Serves 4

"One cannot . . . love well, sleep well, if one has not dined well."
—Virginia Woolf, *A Room of One's Own*

CHICKEN CUTLETS À LA JOANIE

Boneless chicken breasts
Seasoned bread crumbs
Beaten egg
Garlic powder
Lemon pepper
Salt
Butter or oleo

Pound each chicken breast until it is fairly flat (about ¼″ thick). (Shirley uses a favorite, smooth rock from the beach for this procedure.)

Dip chicken in beaten egg and roll in bread crumbs. Arrange chicken on foil-lined cookie sheet. Dot each piece with small amount of butter (or spray with butter-flavored spray), and sprinkle with seasonings to taste.

Bake in preheated 375° oven for approximately 10 minutes. Be careful not to overcook.

Good served with Mushroom and Leek Sauce (see page 168).

A super Joanie Cosselman recipe. The secret is to not overcook the chicken. You may season plain breadcrumbs to suit your taste or use finely crushed, packaged stuffing mix. You can also cook extra breasts in this manner to take for a beach picnic lunch.

—Shirley

ORANGE BAKED CHICKEN

1 chicken, skinned and cut in pieces

Marinade:
6 oz. frozen orange juice concentrate or 1½ cups orange juice
1 tbsp. grated orange rind
2 tbsp. lite soy sauce
1 tbsp. minced onion
¼ cup chopped fresh parsley (1 tsp., dried)
1 clove garlic, minced
¼ tsp. pepper

The Jacksons and Craigs eat a lot of chicken. This marinade is excellent for an oven-baked bird. J.W. cooks this dish in The Double-Minded Men *(reissued as* Vineyard Deceit*).*

—Phil

Combine all ingredients except chicken. Place chicken in a sealable plastic bag. Pour marinade over chicken and marinate in refrigerator overnight.

Remove chicken from marinade and place in greased 9x12″ pan. Pour marinade over chicken. Cover pan and bake for 45 minutes in a preheated 400° oven. Uncover and continue baking until tender. Baste several times with sauce while cooking.

If desired, thicken remaining sauce in pan with cornstarch and serve as gravy.

Serves 6

NEIL'S CHICKEN MARSALA

6 boneless, skinless chicken breast halves, cut into chunks
¼ lb. butter (for frying)—add more if needed
1½ lb. fresh mushrooms, sliced
1½ cups Marsala wine (or use part chicken broth)
Salt and pepper to taste
Flour for dredging

Dredge chicken chunks in flour, and sauté in skillet until nicely browned and cooked. Put chicken in casserole dish and keep warm.

Add wine to drippings in pan. Stir in mushrooms and cook until mushrooms are done and liquid is reduced. You may add a little Wondra flour or corn starch to thicken, if desired, and more wine or broth to increase amount of sauce (optional).

Pour sauce over chicken, mix, and serve in casserole or on a platter, with rice or noodles.

Serves 4–6

Our friend and neighbor Neil Patt is an excellent cook, and J.W. steals his recipes as often as he can. In this recipe, the Marsala elevates the flavor to new heights.

—Zee

ELAINE'S CHICKEN DIVAN

6 boneless chicken breast halves, poached or sautéed and cut in strips
4 10-oz. pkgs. frozen broccoli, cooked and well drained
2 cans cream of chicken soup
1½ cups mayonnaise (or a shade less)
⅔ cups half-and-half
1½ cup grated Cheddar cheese
2 tsp. lemon juice
1 tsp. curry powder
1 cup bread crumbs (buttered)

Elaine Patt served us this excellent dish and gave us the recipe. It serves a crowd and can be frozen. It is a divine divan.

—Shirley

Mix chicken and broccoli together and place in 9x13" casserole dish. Mix remaining ingredients, except bread crumbs, and pour mixture over chicken and broccoli. Cover with bread crumbs and bake at 350° for 40 minutes or until hot.

Serves 6–10

NEIL'S CRISPY ONION CHICKEN

¹/₃–¹/₂ cup melted butter (or oleo)
1 tbsp. Worcestershire sauce
1 tsp. ground mustard
¹/₂ tsp. garlic powder
¹/₄ tsp. pepper
4 chicken breast halves, skinned and boned
1 (6-oz.) can regular or Cheddar-flavored French-fried
onions, crushed

In a shallow bowl, mix together first 5 ingredients. Dip chicken in mixture, then coat with crushed onions. Place in a greased 9″ square baking pan, and top with any remaining onions. Drizzle with any remaining butter mixture, and bake uncovered in a preheated 350° oven for 30–35 minutes or until juices run clear.

Serves 4

Another Neil Patt winner! This recipe appears in the back of Second Sight. *Like many excellent recipes, it's amazingly simple.*

—Shirley

CHICKEN WITH SNOW PEAS

Cooking Sauce:

$^1/_2$ cup water

1 tbsp. dry sherry

2 tbsp. oyster sauce (or soy sauce)

$^1/_4$ tsp. sugar

1 tsp. sesame oil

1 tbsp. cornstarch

Stir together until sauce is well mixed, then set aside.

A taste of Asian cuisine requiring few special ingredients. This recipe is also good with shrimp, if you're tired of chicken. We first printed it in Murder at a Vineyard Mansion.

—J.W.

4 dried Oriental mushrooms (soaked in warm water to cover for 30 minutes)

2 tsp. each of soy sauce, cornstarch, dry sherry, and water

Dash of white pepper

$1^1/_2$ lbs. chicken breasts, skinned, boned, and cut into bite-size pieces

$3^1/_2$ tbsp. peanut oil

1 small clove garlic, minced

$^1/_2$ cup sliced bamboo shoots

$^1/_4$ lb. snow peas (or 6 oz. frozen pea pods, thawed)

Drain mushrooms, discard stems, squeeze caps dry, and thinly slice.

In a bowl, mix together soy sauce, sherry, water, cornstarch, and white pepper. Add chicken to coat, then stir in $1^1/_2$ tsp. of the oil. Let marinate for 15 minutes.

Place wok over high heat and, when hot, add 1 tbsp. of the oil. When oil is hot, add garlic, stir once, and add half of the chicken mixture. Stir-fry until meat is no longer pink in center (about 3 minutes). Remove chicken and set aside. Repeat to cook remaining chicken, adding a little more oil if needed.

Pour remaining tablespoon of oil into wok. When hot, add mushrooms and bamboo shoots. Stir-fry for 1 minute, then add pea pods and stir-fry for 3 minutes (30 seconds if using frozen pea pods), adding a few drops of water if wok is dry. Return chicken to wok. Stir in Cooking Sauce and continue to stir until sauce boils and thickens.

Toasted, blanched almonds or peanuts may be added as a garnish when serving.

Serves 4

SWEET AND SOUR CHICKEN

1 (8-oz.) bottle Wishbone Russian Dressing (the red one)
1 (1³/₈ oz.) envelope dried onion soup mix
1 (10-oz.) jar apricot preserves
Broiler-fryer chicken (cut up)

Combine first 3 ingredients. Place chicken, skin side up, in a single layer in a large, shallow baking pan. Pour sauce over chicken. Bake at 350° for 1–1¹/₂ hours, or until cooked through, basting occasionally with pan drippings. Serve over rice with pan juices.

Serves 8

This is an old recipe that circulated among Shirley's friends many years ago, when all were busy young mothers. It is as good now as it was then!

—Phil

EASY CURRIED CHICKEN

4–8 chicken parts (skinned and boned, if desired)
¼ cup honey or pure maple syrup
2 tsp. prepared Dijon-style mustard
½ tsp. curry powder
¼ cup low-sodium soy sauce

Mix honey, mustard, curry powder, and soy sauce together. Place chicken pieces in baking pan in single layer. Pour sauce over chicken (reserving some to baste chicken after turning). Bake in a preheated 350° oven for 50–60 minutes, turning once halfway through, until cooked through.

Serve over rice with pan juices. Serve with Apricot Chutney (see page 185) or Mango-Cucumber-Green Onion Salsa (see page 178) on the side, or whatever accompaniment you like with curried dishes.

Serves 4

You're bound to have everything on hand required to make this easy recipe. You can certainly add more curry powder to suit your taste.

—Shirley

CHICKEN ENCHILADAS

12 soft tortillas
2 large onions, thinly sliced
2 tbsp. butter
2 cups cooked chicken, diced
$\frac{1}{2}$ cup roasted sweet red peppers (may be purchased in jars)
6 oz. cream cheese, diced
Salt to taste
$\frac{1}{2}$ cup cream or milk
2 cups shredded Jack cheese

In frying pan, cook onions in butter, stirring occasionally, until limp and barely browned (about 20 minutes). Remove from heat and add cooked chicken, peppers, and cream cheese. Mix lightly to blend and salt to taste.

Spoon $\frac{1}{3}$ cup filling down center of each tortilla and roll to enclose. Set, seam side down, in a greased 9x13″ baking dish, side by side (may be covered and refrigerated at this point if making ahead).

Moisten tops of enchiladas with cream, and sprinkle with Jack cheese. Bake uncovered in preheated 375° oven for 20 minutes to heat through (30 minutes if chilled, with casserole covered for first 15 minutes).

Serves 6

J.W. uses French Dessert Crepes (see pages 143 and 144) instead of tortillas when he makes this dish. It's a good idea to make some extras and freeze them for a later date. The recipe may be found at the back of Vineyard Enigma.

—Zee

OVEN-FRIED CHICKEN

Chicken pieces for the number of people you want to serve
(probably at least 2 pieces per person)
Packaged herb stuffing mix (crushed to fine crumbs with a
rolling pin or in food processor)
Canola oil

*Shirl maintains that I
would probably eat my
shoes if I could deep-fat-
fry them. This is a much
easier and less messy way
to eat one of my favorite
foods: fried chicken. We
haven't pan-fried a
chicken for years.*

     —Phil

Skin chicken pieces, if you prefer it that way, and shake in
plastic bag with stuffing mix crumbs. You may, of course,
use fine, dry bread crumbs or tortilla chip crumbs that you
have seasoned to your liking.

Heat a small amount of oil in a baking pan large enough
to hold pieces in 1 layer without crowding, in a 400° oven
until hot. Remove baking pan from oven and place chicken
pieces, in a single layer, in hot oil. Return pan to oven and
bake for about 1 hour, turning pieces once halfway
through. Drain chicken on paper towels.

Cool and refrigerate in covered container if not using
immediately.

This is also good cold and may be made a day ahead if you
want to take it on a beach picnic.

SMOKED TURKEY

1 (10- to 12-lb.) turkey
1 medium onion (quartered)
3–4 stalks celery (cut in chunks)
Salt and pepper
Sage
Hickory chips which have been soaked at least 1 hour in water

Drain hickory chips, place in pan above smoker burner, and heat until smoking.

Rinse turkey, inside and out, with cold water. Rub inside and out with salt, pepper, and ground sage. Fill cavity with onion and celery pieces. Place on top rack of smoker above a pan filled with water (some white wine and seasonings, such as rosemary leaves, may be added to the water). It is best to bring turkey to room temperature before placing in smoker. Smoke according to your smoker directions or until interior of thigh reaches 180°. This could take anywhere from 6–10 hours. Be sure to keep water in pan beneath bird and add hickory chips as needed. Cooking time will depend on outside temperature, number of times smoker is opened, temperature inside smoker, etc. If desired, bird may be removed from smoker before completely done and put in microwave or conventional oven until cooked.

This is an excellent alternative way to prepare your Thanksgiving turkey.

—Phil

Warning: You may become addicted to this way of serving turkey or chicken!

BRINED, GRILLED TURKEY

1 10- to 20-lb. turkey
Stuffing
³/₄ cups kosher (coarse) salt

Brine: In a large container such as a plastic dishpan, fill halfway with cold water, add kosher salt, and stir until mixed. Place turkey in pan; add additional water to cover turkey. Refrigerate 24 hours, turning turkey after 12 hours to ensure that it is evenly brined.

Preheat grill for 10 minutes to 400°–450°.

Rinse turkey and pat dry. Stuff with your favorite stuffing.

Place turkey in disposable roasting pan coated with cooking spray and place a tent of aluminum foil over the bird. Seal tightly. Place bird on grill and reduce heat to 350°–375°.*

Close grill lid and cook for 3 hours (without peeking!).

Remove tent, baste turkey with drippings (saving some for your gravy).

Close grill lid and cook 15 minutes more. Internal meat temperature should be 180°.

Remove bird from grill and allow it to sit for 10 minutes before carving.

Brining a turkey or chicken results in a wonderfully moist meat, whether you grill or roast the bird. Do not brine a kosher turkey because it's already been salted.

—J.W.

* Large turkeys (over 15 lb.) roast more evenly at lower temperatures. 12–14 lb. birds do well at higher heat.

PORK SATE

1½ lb. pork tenderloin
¼ cup butter
1 tbsp. lemon juice
Grated lemon rind from 1 lemon
½ tsp. Tabasco sauce
3 tbsp. grated onion
3 tbsp. light brown sugar
1 tsp. coriander
½ tsp. ground cumin
¼ tsp. ground ginger
1 clove garlic, crushed
½ cup Indonesian Soya sauce or Kikkoman teriyaki sauce
Salt and pepper to taste (go easy on salt)

Cut pork tenderloin into ¾-inch cubes and place in shallow
glass dish. Melt butter in saucepan and add remaining
ingredients. Bring to a boil and simmer 5 minutes. Pour
over meat, cover, and leave overnight in refrigerator. Turn
meat periodically.

Remove meat from marinade (reserve) and put 5 or 6 pieces
on skewer. Grill for 15 minutes or until done, turning
frequently (don't overcook). Meat may also be cooked in
broiler. Reheat marinade and pour over meat. Set skewers
on platter in a bed of rice. Good served with a Peanut
Dipping Sauce (see page 169). Serve with Spinach Salad
(see page 69).

Serves 6–8

*J.W. cooks this in
Death on a Vineyard
Beach. Chicken breasts
may be very successfully
substituted for pork,
if you're a defender or
loather of pigs. If you're
a defender or loather
of chickens, too, you
should probably not
cook this dish.*

—Zee

BRADY'S THANKSGIVING SEA DUCK

A note from Brady Coyne: "Sea ducks have an undeservedly bad reputation as table fare. As a result, J.W.'s duck-hunting friends like to give away what they manage to shoot. I happen to think sea ducks are delish, and J.W. and Zee agree with me. We believe a dinner of sea ducks with all the trimmings is a suitable way to remember our first settlers, who lived off the land and probably considered sea ducks delish, too." This recipe was first printed in the book First Light.

—Brady Coyne

Sea ducks should be prepared the day before you intend to serve them, as you need to marinate the meat for about 36 hours.

Remove the breasts, including the skin, and discard the rest of the ducks. One eider breast feeds 2. With smaller ducks such as old squaw, figure 1 breast per person.

Slice the meat off the breasts. The slices should be about ¹/₂″ thick.

Spread the breast slices in a high-sided platter and cover with milk. Cover the platter with aluminum foil and marinate in the refrigerator all day, for about 12 hours. The evening before your feast, drain off the milk, rinse the meat, pat it dry on paper towels, then cover again in fresh milk and marinate overnight, 8–12 hours. The 2 rounds of milk marinade will neutralize the gaminess and bring out the distinctive flavor of sea ducks.

The morning before you plan to serve the ducks, drain off the milk, rinse and pat dry again, and cover the meat with a robust red wine. Let the meat marinate in the refrigerator for about 6 hours.

Drain the meat and pat dry with paper towels. Do not rinse this time.

Rub both sides of the meat with salt, freshly ground black pepper, ground red pepper, dried sage, and rosemary.

In a very hot skillet, coated with olive oil, sear the meat on both sides. Do not overcook. It should be rare on the inside.

Serve with cranberry sauce or chutney, wild rice, fresh green vegetables (steamed asparagus would be my choice, but it's not in season in New England in November), a green salad and an excellent red wine.

ORANGE VENISON ROAST

1 medium venison roast
2–3 slices bacon (cut into small pieces)
2 smashed garlic cloves
1 bay leaf
2 whole cloves
Salt and pepper
1 cup orange juice

If you're a hunter or know one who'll share his take with you, try this venison roast. Remember that the secret to preparing wild game is to not overcook it. J.W. cooks this in Off Season.

—Shirley

Cut slits in roast and insert pieces of bacon, garlic, salt, and pepper. Sear meat in hot, lightly oiled skillet. Place roast on rack in uncovered roasting pan and top with bay leaf and cloves. Place in preheated 450° oven and immediately reduce heat to 350°. Roast to internal temperature of 140–150°, basting frequently with orange juice (about 20–25 minutes per pound). Serve with pan gravy or Cumberland Sauce (see page 175).

6–8 servings per 7- to 8-lb. roast

BEEF WELLINGTON

Whenever I cook this splendid dish, I'm reminded of the time I prepared it for my then very picky teenaged son, who considered a Big Mac to be the world's best meal and who would eat very little of what I cooked. Frustrated, I made a Beef Wellington, put a slab of it on his plate, and said, "Taste that! Even you will like Beef Wellington!" He eyed it suspiciously, then took a tiny bite. "Well," I said triumphantly, "what do you think?" He chewed slowly, then shook his head, stifled a sneer, and said, "I don't like soft meat." I'm happy to report that now that he's grown up and become a human being, he's changed his mind.

—Phil

Note: Recipes for Pate Brisee, Sauce Perigueux, and Chicken Liver Pate all follow.

Make 2¹/₂ recipes pate brisee

4-lb. beef fillet, trimmed
1 cup burgundy
1 cup sherry
1 onion, quartered
2 bay leaves
³/₄ stick of butter, softened
Salt
Pepper
2 7¹/₂-oz. tins mouse de foie gras (or chicken liver pate, or a good quality liverwurst)
1 egg

Marinate a 4-lb. beef fillet, trimmed, overnight in a mixture of 1 cup burgundy, 1 cup sherry, 1 quartered onion, and 2 bay leaves. Remove beef from marinade in the morning. Tie fillet crosswise at 1-inch intervals with kitchen string, spread fillet with ³/₄ stick butter, softened, and sprinkle with salt and pepper. Roast the beef on a rack in a roasting pan in a pre-heated 450° oven for 15 minutes. Let the beef cool completely on the rack, remove and discard string, and chill the beef, wrapped in plastic wrap, for 30 minutes.

Roll out the dough (pate brisee) ¹/₈″ thick on a floured surface, cut out a rectangle just large enough to enclose the beef (about 24x12″), and reserve the trimmings.

In a food processor fitted with the steel blade, or in a blender, puree the mouse de foie gras and spread it on the beef. (**Note:** Chicken liver pate or liverwurst may be substituted.)

Arrange the beef in the center of the dough and wrap the dough around it. Moisten the edges of the dough with water and pinch them together to seal them. Pinch off any excess dough from the ends and transfer the Wellington, seam side down, to a baking sheet. Decorate the Wellington with shapes cut from the reserved dough, attaching the shapes with an egg wash (made by lightly beating 1 egg with 1 tbsp. water) and chill the Wellington, loosely covered, for 30 minutes or until the dough is firm.

Cut several small vents in the dough, brush the dough with the remaining egg wash, and bake the Wellington in the lower third of a preheated 450° oven for 30 minutes or until it is golden brown. Transfer the Wellington to a heated platter, cut it into thick slices, and serve it with Sauce Perigueux.

Serves 6 (at least)

PATE BRISEE

1¹/₄ cups flour
³/₄ stick cold butter, cut into bits
2 tbsp. shortening
¹/₄ tsp. salt
3 tbsp. water

In a large bowl, blend 1¹/₄ cups flour, ³/₄ stick cold butter cut into bits, 2 tbsp. shortening, and ¹/₄ tsp. salt until mixture resembles meal. Add 3 tbsp. water, and toss the mixture until the water is incorporated, then form the dough into a ball. Knead the dough lightly with the heel of the hand against a smooth surface for a few seconds to distribute the fat evenly, and re-form it into a ball. Dust the dough with flour and chill it, wrapped in plastic wrap, for 1 hour.

SAUCE PERIGUEUX

2 cups beef broth
2 tsp. arrowroot
3 tbsp. cold water
$^1/_3$ cup Madeira
1 tbsp. truffle, minced
Truffle liquor
1 tbsp. butter

In a saucepan bring 2 cups of beef broth to a boil over moderately high heat, and simmer it for 15 minutes.

Dissolve 2 tsp. arrowroot in 3 tbsp. cold water; add the mixture to the stock and simmer, stirring, until the sauce has thickened. Cook until reduced to about 1 cup, add $^1/_3$ cup Madeira, bring sauce to just a boil. This is a Madeira sauce. To make Sauce Perigueux, combine the Madeira sauce with 1 tbsp. minced truffle and a little of the truffle liquor. Simmer over low heat for 5 minutes and swirl in 1 tbsp. of butter.

If you don't want to re-mortgage the house, Madeira sauce will do just fine.

CHICKEN LIVER PATE

3 slices bacon
1 medium yellow onion, chopped (about 1 cup)
2 carrots, grated
2 large cloves garlic, minced
2 tbsp. butter
1 lb. chicken livers (free range if possible), trimmed of fat and rinsed
2 tbsp. cognac
1½ tsp. kosher salt
1 tsp. freshly ground pepper
Pinch nutmeg
½ cup fresh parsley, chopped
¼–½ cup heavy cream (optional)
Parsley for garnish

This is an elegant substitute for mousse (or pate) de foie gras and doesn't torture any geese. The recipe makes enough for the Beef Wellington entrée with enough left over to serve with toast rounds for hors d'oeuvres.

—Shirley

In large skillet, cook bacon over moderate heat until browned (about 5 minutes). Add onions and cook until they are transparent and golden. Add carrots, garlic, and butter and cook until carrots are tender. Add chicken livers and cognac and cook, stirring gently, until livers are cooked through but still slightly pink in the center (about 6–8 minutes). Season with salt, pepper, and nutmeg. Add chopped parsley, stir, and remove from heat. Place mixture in a food processor and process until smooth. Heavy cream may be added at this time if you prefer a creamier consistency.

After cooling, divide pate between small ramekins for serving purposes. Refrigerate for up to 5 days. Ramekins may also be wrapped in plastic wrap and then in aluminum foil and frozen for later use. Serve garnished with sprigs of parsley, and surround with toasted bread or plain crackers.

Makes about 3 cups

MEDALLIONS OF BEEF IN COGNAC CREAM

4 (4-oz.) beef tenderloin steaks
Salt and cracked pepper
2 tbsp. olive oil
2 tbsp. unsalted butter
2 shallots or 1 small onion, chopped
$^1/_4$ cup cognac
$^1/_2$ cup whipping cream
Fresh parsley for garnish

A simple, elegant recipe. The steaks ooze flavor and melt in your mouth. You can substitute sirloin tips for the tenderloins and use half-and-half instead of the cream, but don't leave out the cognac!

—Shirley

Sprinkle steaks with salt and pepper. Combine oil and butter in a large skillet and heat over medium heat until butter melts. Add the steaks and cook 5 minutes on each side. Remove steaks to a serving platter and keep warm.

Drain all but 2 tbsp. of drippings from skillet. Sauté shallots in drippings until tender. Add cognac and cook over medium heat, deglazing skillet by scraping particles that cling to bottom. Gradually stir in whipping cream and cook until heated. Pour sauce over steaks and garnish with parsley.

Note: Less expensive cuts of beef (such as sirloin tips) can be used in place of tenderloin with good results.

Serves 4

TOM'S SAUSAGE, BEANS, AND RICE

$^2/_3$–$^3/_4$ lb. smoked sausage (like kielbasa), split lengthwise
and cut into 2″ lengths
1 large onion, finely chopped
2 cloves garlic, chopped
2 tbsp. olive oil
1 tsp. dried oregano leaves
$^1/_2$ tsp. dried basil leaves
Dash Tabasco
2 (1-lb.) cans red beans (drained or not as desired)

Heat oil in skillet. Brown sausage. Remove sausage from
pan, and sauté onion and garlic until soft. Add remaining
ingredients and sausage. Cover and simmer over low heat
for about 30 minutes. Mash a few of the beans during the
last 5 minutes. Serve over rice.

Serves 4

*This recipe may be
found in* A Vineyard
Killing. *Definitely drain
the canned beans! Who
needs all that sodium?
And the end result is
better without the bean
slime. Add a little water
or dry red wine if you
desire more liquid.*

—Zee

*Make sure that you use
all of the juice in the
canned beans! The juice
makes all the difference
between a good dish and
an exceptional one! Dr.
Thomas Blues, who gave
us this recipe, always
uses the bean juice! If
you can't trust a doctor,
whom can you trust?*

—J.W.

BLACK BEAN CHILI

1 tbsp. olive oil
1 large onion, chopped
1 sweet green pepper, diced
1 clove garlic, minced
$\frac{1}{2}$ lb. ground turkey
$\frac{1}{4}$ cup chili powder (or to taste)
1 tbsp. ground cumin
$\frac{1}{4}$ tsp. salt
$\frac{1}{2}$ tsp. ground allspice
1 (16-oz.) can crushed tomatoes
1 cup water
2 (15-oz.) cans black beans, drained and rinsed
4 oz. chopped green chilies
1 can corn kernels (or hominy)*
2 cups cooked pasta—small shells or spirals (optional)
Shredded Cheddar cheese
Chopped scallions

A Shirley original enjoyed by even "chili purists," whatever they are. Nothing warms up a winter day like a bowl of this hearty chili. Be sure to make enough for leftovers or the freezer.

—Phil

Heat oil in large skillet or Dutch oven. Sauté onion, green pepper, and garlic until softened but not brown (about 8 minutes). Add ground turkey and cook until meat is no longer pink (about 5 minutes).

Stir in spices and salt. Sauté 1 minute. Add tomatoes and water. Simmer 7 minutes.

Stir in beans, green chilies, and corn or hominy. Simmer, stirring occasionally, about 10 minutes. Add cooked pasta (if using) and heat until warm.

Serve in bowls and garnish with shredded cheese, or sour cream, and chopped scallions.

*Kuner's Southwestern Pepi Hominy with sweet peppers is good.

Good served with hot corn muffins or Raised Mexican Cornbread (see page 200).

Serves 6

LINGUINI WITH SHELLFISH AND GARLIC SAUCE

2–3 dozen quahogs (hard-shelled New England clams) or
equivalent amount of shrimp, scallops, or mussels*
6 tbsp. butter
2 cloves garlic, finely chopped
1 shallot, finely chopped
1/4 cup dry white wine
Generous pinch dried thyme
Freshly ground pepper
Salt, if needed
1 lb. linguini, cooked according to package directions

Steam quahogs in 1/2 cup water over high heat, just until
shellfish open. Cool, remove quahogs from shells, and chop
coarsely. Reserve 1/4–1/2 cup broth.

Melt butter in heavy saucepan. Add garlic and shallot and
sauté until soft. Add chopped quahogs and broth to taste,
along with wine, thyme, and pepper. Heat through gently.
Serve over cooked linguini with freshly grated Parmesan
cheese.

Serves 4

* If using mussels, steam them in the same manner. Shrimp
or scallops should be lightly sautéed.

*Jeff sometimes brings
home more quahogs
than the Jacksons and
their guests can eat on
the half-shell, as casinos,
or as stuffers, or than
he can use as chowder
makings. (There are lots
of quahogs in Edgartown
ponds!) This is a good
way to use the extra
ones. Serve with a fresh
green salad and some
crusty bread to dip in
flavored olive oil.*

—Zee

PASTA WITH SALMON

8-12 oz. spinach noodles, cooked according to package directions and drained
3 tbsp. unsalted butter
4 oz. sliced mushrooms
8 oz. salmon, cooked and flaked (a good use for the leftovers)
1-1½ cups asparagus, cooked to crisp tender and sliced diagonally
½ cup freshly grated Parmesan cheese
½ tsp. ground nutmeg
1 cup dairy sour cream
Paprika

You may substitute edible pod peas (or tiny frozen peas) for the asparagus in this recipe. If you want to go all out, pass some Mustard Cream Sauce (see page 171) to which you've added some snipped fresh dill and a few capers.

—Shirley

Melt butter in Dutch oven (or large saucepan). Saute mushrooms until they've released their juices. Add salmon, asparagus, cheese, and nutmeg to pot and heat gently over low heat. Add noodles, stirring gently, until hot. Fold in sour cream and heat just until hot (add a bit of milk if sauce needs thinning). Spoon into a heated serving dish and sprinkle with paprika.

Serves 4-6

SPINACH LASAGNA

1-lb. pkg. of wide egg noodles
2 (10-oz.) pkgs. frozen chopped spinach (cooked and well drained)
½ lb. sliced mushrooms
1 large onion, diced
2 cloves minced garlic
½ sweet green pepper, diced
1 lb. Ricotta cheese
½ cup grated Parmesan cheese
1 tsp. salt
½ tsp. dried oregano
½ tsp. pepper
¼ tsp. nutmeg
3 cups spaghetti sauce
12 oz. Mozzarella cheese, shredded

Shirley and our daughter Kim have an ongoing contest concerning whose lasagna weighs the most. That may not seem like a meaningful criterion for quality to you, but it supports the theory that you can't have too much of a good thing.

—Phil

Cook noodles al dente and drain. Sauté onions, garlic, mushrooms, and green pepper in a little olive oil and add with cooked spinach to noodles. Add Ricotta and Parmesan cheese, salt, pepper, nutmeg, oregano, and 2 cups spaghetti sauce. Pour mixture into buttered 9x13″ baking dish (or two 9x9″ pans). Top with remaining sauce and Mozzarella cheese. Bake at 350° for 30 minutes or until heated through.

May be frozen, well covered. (Cover lasagna with plastic wrap before wrapping again in aluminum foil. Defrost, and don't forget to remove the plastic wrap before reheating.)

Serves 8–12

PAELLA A LA VALENCIANA

1 small chicken, stewed, boned, and cut into pieces
(Save 2¼ cups broth)
8 pork sausages cut into bite-size chunks (use hot chicken or turkey sausages, if you prefer)
½ lb. cleaned squid (or shrimp)
1 small onion, finely chopped
3 cloves garlic, finely chopped
3 tomatoes, seeded, peeled, and chopped
2 sweet peppers, any color, seeded and chopped
6 canned artichoke hearts
A few mussels or small quahogs (hard-shelled New England clams)
½ cup peas
1 tsp. paprika
½ tsp. saffron
½ cup olive oil
Salt and pepper
1 cup rice
2 eggs, hard-boiled and sliced—to be used as garnish, if desired
Ripe olives, sliced—to be used as garnish, if desired

We first had this colorful version of paella while living in Spain in 1973, and it's still our favorite. Years later, our daughter Kim requested that it be served at her wedding. It can be cooked and attractively presented in a paella pan, though that traditional pan isn't necessary. All of the seafood can be harvested in Vineyard ponds or purchased from local fish markets. The recipe was published in Vineyard Enigma.

—Shirley

If possible, use a paella pan; otherwise use a large skillet. This recipe makes a lot of paella; if you're only serving 4–6 people, cut way back on the ingredients.

Heat the pan, add the oil, and cook the sausages. Add garlic, onion, peppers, and tomatoes, and let them brown. Add paprika, then add rice, allowing it to brown slightly as you stir, then add 2¼ cups boiling broth. Add chicken. Add saffron; add salt and pepper to taste and stir everything. Cook on high heat for about 5 minutes, then turn the heat down to moderate for 10–15 minutes. Add seafood, artichokes, and peas, and cook until rice is tender (about 5–10 more minutes). If you have to add some more fluid, use the remaining broth or juice from other ingredients. I use a spatula to scrape the bottom of the pan and turn its contents from time to time during cooking, just in case I have my heat too high.

All ingredients except the rice can be prepared the day before, but the broth you use to cook the rice must be boiling hot. After the paella is cooked, let it rest for 5 or 10 minutes so it will soak up any excess broth.

Note: Part of the sweet peppers can be sliced and used as a garnish, along with the sliced hard-boiled eggs and sliced olives.

Serves 8

SAROFIMIAN BHAJJI

2 medium-size eggplants (about $1/2$ lb. each)
6 oz. mustard oil or butter
1 tsp. powdered turmeric
$1/2$ tsp. chili powder
Salt to taste

Here is another way to serve eggplant. Your guests will be impressed with your ethnic expertise. J.W. cooks this dish in The Double-Minded Men, *reissued as* Vineyard Deceit.

—Phil

Wash the eggplants and slice them (unpeeled) into rounds no more than $1/8''$ thick. Steep them in cold water for an hour, then remove and pat dry.

Mix turmeric, salt, and chili powder into a paste with a little water and apply to both sides of eggplant slices.

Pour the oil into a large frying pan and heat until oil begins to smoke. Fry eggplant slices (in batches) until golden brown and tender, turning slices to brown both sides. Keep warm until all slices are fried.

When done, place in a warm dish and eat with plain boiled rice accompanied by an Indian-type chutney. Also good served with Indian flat bread.

Serves 4

MOUSSAKA

*A Greek staple and
a delicious way to
showcase those
eggplants when they
become abundant in
your garden or at the
Farmers Market.
A Greek salad and
dolmas make nice
accompaniments.
Try Taramosalata
(see page 28) with
toasted pita wedges as
an appetizer, egg-lemon
soup as a first course,
and baklava for dessert.*

—Shirley

2 medium eggplants (1½–2 lbs.)
Salt
½ lb. lean ground beef
½ lb. ground lamb
1 cup chopped onion
⅓ cup tomato paste
¼ cup snipped parsley
¼ cup dry red wine
¼ cup water
2 beaten eggs
¼ cup grated Parmesan cheese
¼ cup fine, dry breadcrumbs
¾ tsp. salt
½ tsp. ground cinnamon
⅛ tsp. pepper

Sauce (or use Béchamel sauce)
4 tbsp. unsalted butter
¼ cup flour
¼ tsp. salt
Dash pepper
Dash ground nutmeg
2 cups milk
2 slightly beaten egg yolks
2 tbsp. lemon juice
***
Cooking oil
¼ cup fine, dry breadcrumbs
2 tbsp. grated Parmesan cheese
1 tbsp. butter, melted

Pare eggplant; cut crosswise into ³/₄″ slices. Sprinkle slices with a little salt; set aside.

In skillet, cook ground meats and onion until meat is browned and onion is tender. Drain off excess fat. Add tomato paste, parsley, wine, and water. Simmer, uncovered, for 5 minutes; cool. Stir in eggs, the ¹/₄ cup cheese, the first ¹/₄ cup breadcrumbs, ³/₄ tsp. salt, the cinnamon, and pepper; set aside.

In medium saucepan, prepare sauce: Melt the 4 tbsp. butter. Blend in flour, remaining salt, pepper, and nutmeg. Add milk all at once. Cook and stir until thickened and bubbly. Stir about 1 cup hot mixture into egg yolks. Return all to saucepan and cook, stirring constantly, for 2 minutes. Remove from heat and gradually stir in lemon juice. Set aside.

Rinse and dry eggplant slices and lightly brush with cooking oil. Brown, in hot skillet, on both sides. Drain on paper toweling.

Grease a 12x7x2″ baking dish and sprinkle bottom with 2 tbsp. remaining bread crumbs. Layer with half the eggplant, then layer with the meat combination; repeat layers, ending with sauce. Sprinkle each layer with breadcrumbs and Parmesan cheese if desired. Pour sauce over all.

Bake, covered, in a preheated 350° oven for 45 minutes. Combine remaining breadcrumbs, Parmesan, and melted butter. Uncover; sprinkle crumbs over moussaka. Return to oven and bake, uncovered, for 15 minutes more.

Makes 6–8 servings

SPANAKOPITA (Greek Spinach Pie)

8 oz. unsalted butter

1 bunch scallions, chopped

2 (10-oz.) pkg. frozen, chopped spinach

6 eggs, lightly beaten

8 oz. Feta cheese, crumbled

8 oz. cottage cheese

2 tbsp. farina (cream of wheat)

$^1/_2$ cup fresh parsley, chopped

$^1/_4$ cup fresh dill, chopped

$^1/_2$ tsp. salt

$^1/_4$ tsp. pepper

1 pkg. phyllo pastry dough (about 1 lb.) thawed

This Greek delicacy can be cut into small triangles and served as an appetizer or cut into larger squares and served with souvlakia and Greek potatoes.

—Zee

Melt butter in small saucepan. Butter a 13x9″ baking dish. Preheat oven to 375°.

Sauté scallions in 2 tbsp. butter in large skillet until tender. Cook spinach in large saucepan or in microwave, following label directions. Drain, pressing out as much liquid as possible.

Combine onions, spinach, eggs, Feta, cottage cheese, farina, herbs, and seasonings in a large bowl.

Unfold phyllo pastry leaves, and place between damp towels to keep from drying. Remove pastry 1 sheet at a time and place in baking dish. Brush each sheet with melted butter. (Cut pastry to fit baking dish if necessary.) Repeat until there are 6 layers of buttered pastry.

Spread spinach mixture evenly over the pastry.

Butter and stack 8 more sheets of phyllo on top of spinach mixture. Mark pastry lightly into 12 squares with sharp knife. Do not cut all the way through.

Place spanakopita in preheated oven. Immediately lower temperature to 350°. Bake for about 1 hour, or until golden brown and puffed. Cool slightly before cutting into squares.

Makes 12 servings

FRENCH CREPES

4 eggs
2 cups milk
2 cups flour
Pinch salt
$^1/_4$ cup melted butter

Beat eggs and milk in medium-sized bowl with electric mixer until blended. Add flour and salt and beat until smooth. Stir in butter. Refrigerate at least 30 minutes. Batter should be the consistency of heavy cream.

Heat a 5–6″ skillet or crepe pan. When hot, grease very lightly (a quick spritz of butter-flavored spray is good). Pour about 2 tbsp. batter into pan, rotating pan quickly to spread batter evenly. Brown crepe lightly on one side, then turn and brown on second side. Stack cooked crepes between rounds of waxed paper while proceeding with remaining batter.

Fill crepes as desired (spinach and seafood crepe fillings follow), and cook according to directions for each recipe.

Makes about 24 crepes

These crepes are the ones used for both the Spinach-Cheese and the Seafood Crepe entrée recipes in this book. The dessert crepes listed below are used for J.W.'s Chicken Enchiladas (see page 121). Dishes made with both of these types of crepes are popular with our dinner guests and can be made ahead of time and frozen, so that you'll have more time for playing host or hostess.

—Shirley

FRENCH DESSERT CREPES

*J.W. prefers this recipe
for all purposes.*

—Zee

Use previous recipe, but add 4 tbsp. powdered sugar and
1 tsp. vanilla to batter.

SPINACH-CHEESE CREPES

French Crepes
2 pkg. (10 oz. each) frozen, chopped spinach, thawed, and
squeezed to remove as much water as possible
1/2 cup shredded Swiss cheese
1/2 cup freshly grated Parmesan cheese
1/3 cup butter
1/4 cup flour
1/2 tsp. salt
1/4 tsp. pepper
1/4 tsp. ground nutmeg
1³/4 cups milk

*One of the many fine
dishes you can make
with crepes. We like this
one because we're
spinach freaks. They can
be served as luncheon
dishes or as side dishes.*

—Phil

Melt butter in large saucepan. Stir in flour, salt, pepper, and
nutmeg. Cook until bubbly (about 1″). Stir in milk and cook,
stirring constantly, until sauce thickens and bubbles. Cook
an additional 2 minutes. Stir in spinach and cheeses and
stir until Swiss cheese is melted.

Fill each crepe with about 1/3 cup filling. Roll up and arrange,
seam side down, in shallow, buttered baking pan. Brush tops
with melted butter and sprinkle with additional Parmesan
cheese. Crepes may be covered well and frozen at this point.
Thaw before baking.

Bake in preheated 375° oven for 15 minutes or until heated
through.

Makes 12 crepes

SEAFOOD CREPES

French Crepes (see page 143)
2 tbsp. melted butter
2 tbsp. flour
1¼ cups milk
3 tbsp. dry sherry
1 tsp. instant chicken bouillon granules
½ tsp. salt
Dash of Cajun seafood seasoning
¼ tsp. crushed red pepper
1 cup shredded Swiss or Gruyere cheese
¼ cup each of minced, sweet red pepper and onion, sautéed
2 cups sliced mushrooms, lightly sautéed
3–4 oz. small shelled and deveined shrimp
6–8 oz. small bay scallops
2 tbsp. toasted and buttered bread crumbs
Parsley sprigs and lemon wedges for garnish

Another excellent crepe dish. It's rich with cheese and seafood of various kinds.

—Shirley

Melt butter in 2-qt. saucepan over medium heat. Stir in flour, cook, and stir for 1 minute. Gradually whisk in milk, sherry, bouillon granules, and seasonings. Cook, stirring constantly, until smooth and thickened. Gradually add cheese. Cook and stir until smooth. Gradually stir in seafood, peppers, onions, and mushrooms. Cook, stirring gently, just until seafood is cooked through (8–10 minutes). Reserve ¾-cup filling.

Fill each crepe with about ⅓ cup filling. Roll up and place, seam side down, in shallow, buttered baking dish. Spoon reserved filling over tops and sprinkle with bread crumbs. Crepes may be covered well and frozen at this point. Thaw before proceeding.

Bake in preheated 375° oven for about 10 minutes or until heated through. Garnish with parsley and lemon wedges.

Makes about 12 crepes; serves 6

SOUVLAKIA

2 lbs. lean lamb (or beef), cubed
2 bay leaves, crumbled
2 tbsp. olive oil
Juice of ¹/₂ lemon (about ¹/₄ cup)
3 cloves garlic, crushed
1 tsp. oregano
Salt and pepper to taste
1 tsp. Colman's Mustard (dry)

This dish is delicious served with pilaf or Greek Potatoes and a Greek Salad. It's also sold by street vendors in Greece as a snack.

—Phil

Marinate cubed meat in sauce, made from remaining ingredients, for at least 30 minutes (or overnight). Remove from marinade and thread on six 12″-long metal skewers with bits of bay leaf in between pieces. Grill over red-hot coals, turning often so that meat is well seared on the outside and tender and juicy inside. Serve at once, accompanied by lemon wedges to squeeze over meat.

Serves 6

GREEK POTATOES

6 medium potatoes (about 3 lbs.), cubed
$^1/_4$ cup fresh lemon juice (gradually add more if desired)
$^1/_3$ cup vegetable oil
1 tbsp. olive oil
2 tsp. salt
$^1/_2$ tsp. black pepper
$1^1/_2$ tsp. dried oregano leaves
2 garlic cloves, minced
3 cups hot water
Fresh Italian parsley, chopped

Toss the potatoes with next 7 ingredients and spread in a deep 9x12″ pan. Add the hot water and bake at 475°, uncovered, for about $1^1/_2$ hrs. Stir every 20 minutes, adding water if necessary to prevent burning or sticking. Watch especially carefully during the last 30 minutes. Allow the water to evaporate until only the oil is left.

Transfer to a serving bowl and garnish with chopped parsley. These are also good sprinkled with crumbled Feta cheese and may be further garnished with strips of roasted red peppers.

Serves 6

These potatoes go very well with Greek Souvlakia. We are very fond of Greek cuisine, so mealtimes were always a welcome event during our visits to that favorite country of ours.

—Phil

Side Dishes

"ASPARAGUS OUT OF THE GARDEN IS
SO TENDER THAT IT REALLY DOESN'T
HAVE TO BE COOKED AT ALL,
BUT ON THE OTHER HAND, A BIT
OF BUTTER DOESN'T HURT IT."

—J.W., IN *VINEYARD FEAR*

(ISSUED FIRST AS *CLIFF HANGER*)

ZEE'S ASPARAGUS

This is my favorite way to cook asparagus. I know that rumors persist that microwaves destroy some vitamin content in food, but until there is more evidence for this theory I'll continue to use this method because of the bright green, perfectly cooked spears it produces.

—Zee

2 lbs. fresh asparagus
2 tbsp. butter or margarine
¼ cup water
Lemon pepper seasoning

Wash and trim asparagus. Place spears in flat, glass baking dish with tips toward center of dish and thicker portions facing ends of dish. Dot with butter and sprinkle with lemon pepper seasoning. Add water and cover with plastic wrap, leaving a vent hole. Microwave at full power for 10–12 minutes (rearranging spears once) or until crisp tender. Let stand, covered, for 2 minutes. Drain and serve.

Serves 6

NATURAL ASPARAGUS

J.W. cooks this in A Beautiful Place to Die. He knows no better way to cook asparagus. It takes a little longer than Zee's method, but produces excellent results.

—Phil

1½ lbs. fresh asparagus
3 tbsp. butter or margarine
Salt and lemon pepper to taste

Rinse and trim asparagus, peeling only very tough portions. Place in 1 or 2 layers in a flat baking dish just large enough to hold stalks. Dot with butter and sprinkle with salt and lemon pepper. Cover tightly with aluminum foil and bake in preheated 300° oven for 30 minutes.

Serves 4–6

BROCCOLI PUFF

2 tbsp. minced onion
$^{1}/_{3}$ cup butter or oleo
$^{1}/_{3}$ cup flour
3 cups milk
2 eggs, slightly beaten
2 tsp. salt
$^{1}/_{8}$ tsp. pepper
3 cups (1$^{1}/_{2}$ lb.) minced broccoli (or about 2 10-oz. pkgs.
frozen, chopped broccoli)
Shredded Mexican or Jack cheese
Canned onion rings or toasted pumpkin seeds
Bacon bits, crumbled, for garnish, if desired

Sauté onion in butter in heavy saucepan until tender. Stir
in flour. Remove from heat and stir in milk. Return to heat
and cook, stirring constantly, until thickened.

Stir small amount into eggs, then stir eggs into sauce. Add
salt, pepper, and broccoli, and mix well. Turn into greased
1$^{1}/_{2}$-qt. casserole. Spread a thin layer of shredded cheese
over all. Sprinkle top with crushed onion rings or toasted
seeds. Bake in preheated 350° oven 40 minutes or until
knife inserted near center comes out clean. Scatter bacon
bits over the top, if desired.

Let stand 5 minutes to set before serving.

Serves 6

*Both the Jacksons and
the Craigs eat a lot of
broccoli because, unlike
George Bush, they like
it. This is a fairly fancy
way to prepare one of
their favorite vegetables.*
—Phil

LEMON-SESAME BROCCOLI

1 head broccoli (about 1½ lbs.)
2 tsp. Oriental sesame oil
1 tbsp. fresh lemon juice
Toasted sesame seeds

Trim flowerets from broccoli head and separate into pieces. Peel stems and cut into ½"-thick rounds.

Fresh broccoli prepared in this way may also be cooked in the same manner as Zee's Asparagus, then stir-fried with the remaining ingredients in a skillet just before serving.

—J.W.

Bring 1" water to boil in large saucepan. Add stem pieces, cover and cook 5 minutes. Add flowerets, cover and cook 5 minutes more or until crisp tender. If this is done well before serving time, drain broccoli, rinse under cold water, and refrigerate.

To serve: Toss hot broccoli in sesame oil and lemon juice. (To reheat chilled broccoli: heat sesame oil in skillet, add broccoli, and stir-fry until heated through.) Add lemon juice and serve sprinkled with toasted sesame seeds.

Serves 4

GINGERED CARROTS

1 lb. carrots, peeled and sliced (or use peeled baby carrots)
3 tbsp. butter
2 tbsp. brown sugar (or maple syrup, if desired)
1½ tsp. ground ginger

A colorful and tasty accompaniment to many entrées. Maple syrup may be substituted for the brown sugar. Even the kids will love these carrots.

Parboil carrots just until crisp tender and drain. Melt butter in heavy skillet. Turn carrots into skillet, and sprinkle with brown sugar and ginger. Stir to coat well with butter, and heat until carrots are hot and done to your liking.

Serves 6

—Shirley

JULIENNE BEETS AND CARROTS

1½ lb. beets, trimmed, leaving 1" of stems attached
1½ lb. large carrots, peeled
3 tbsp. butter
Salt and pepper to taste

John Skye, using J.W.'s recipe, cooks this in Cliff Hanger, *reissued as* Vineyard Fear. *This is a simple and colorful dish, particularly good for winter holiday meals. Even people who profess to dislike beets like them in this combination.*

Simmer beets in water to cover until tender. Drain, rinse, peel, trim, and pat dry with paper towels. Do the same with the carrots.

Julienne beets and carrots by hand or with coarse grating blade in a food processor. Sauté vegetables together in skillet with butter, stirring gently over moderate heat for 4–5 minutes until warm. Salt and pepper to taste.

Serves 6

—Phil

SESAME SNOW PEAS

3 tbsp. sesame oil
1 lb. snow peas, trimmed
10 thin scallions, white bulb and 2″ of green
2 tbsp. pine nuts
1 tbsp. sesame seeds (toasted)
Salt and pepper to taste

The Jacksons and the Craigs prefer these peas to the regular kind. They are tender and good and can be cooked as a part of many wok dishes.

—Phil

Heat oil in large skillet. Add peas and scallions and sauté over medium heat, tossing frequently, for about 3 minutes. Add pine nuts, sesame seeds, salt, and pepper. Cook, stirring, an additional 2–3 minutes. Serve immediately.

Serves 4

EDIBLE POD PEAS

Just one way to serve these welcome early vegetables, if you can refrain from eating them all right off the vine. Joshua and Diana see to it that a goodly amount never reaches the kitchen.

—J.W.

A variety of methods may be used to cook edible pod peas:

First, wash, snap off stem ends, and string if necessary, then

Steam over boiling water until crisp tender, or

Boil, partially covered (to retain color) until crisp tender, or

Heat a small amount of peanut oil in skillet or wok and stir fry over relatively high heat until crisp tender.

CREAMED SPINACH

2 cups steamed spinach
1 1/2–2 tbsp. butter
1 tbsp. finely chopped onion
1 tbsp. flour
1/2 cup hot cream
1/2 tsp. sugar
Salt and pepper
Freshly grated nutmeg or lemon rind

Spinach has to be one of the world's most versatile vegetables. It goes with almost everything and can be prepared in so many ways.

—Shirley

Chop spinach finely. Melt butter in skillet (which may be rubbed with a garlic clove) and sauté onion until golden. Stir in flour until well blended, then slowly stir in cream and sugar. When sauce is hot and smooth, add spinach. Stir and cook about 3 minutes. Season with salt and pepper and grated nutmeg or lemon rind.

Serves 2–4

MEEM'S SPINACH

1 large onion, sliced
3 pkg. frozen, chopped spinach (thawed and drained very well)
2 tbsp. butter
2 tbsp. dry sherry
1/2 cup heavy cream
Salt and pepper to taste

Our dear friend Mimi Adams shared this recipe with us, and we've named it for her.

—Phil

Sauté onion slices in butter until translucent and lightly browned. Add remaining ingredients, heat until spinach is just tender, and serve.

Serves 6

CREAMED SPINACH IN ZUCCHINI BOATS

6 medium zucchini
$^1/_2$ lb. frozen chopped spinach, thawed and squeezed of liquid
$^1/_2$ cup Ricotta cheese
$^1/_4$ tsp. ground nutmeg
1 egg, beaten
2 slices bacon, cooked until crisp and crumbled
$^1/_2$ cup grated Cheddar cheese
Paprika

When the attack of the zucchini monsters reaches your house, you can eat at least six of them in this recipe. The problem with zucchini recipes, of course, is that there are always more zucchinis than recipes. You can scoop out the zucchini seeds, if they're too large, before chopping the pulp. If you prefer, you can also fill the scooped-out shells with defrosted spinach soufflé and cook until the soufflé has set.

—Shirley

Trim ends from zucchini and drop into saucepan of boiling water to cover. Cook 8–10 minutes, or just until tender. Drain and halve lengthwise. Scoop out centers, leaving shells with a little flesh. Finely chop scooped-out flesh.

Mix drained and squeezed spinach with chopped zucchini, Ricotta, nutmeg, and egg. Spoon into zucchini shells and top with combined bacon and cheese. Sprinkle with paprika. Place on greased cookie sheet and bake in preheated 350° oven for 15–20 minutes or until golden.

Serves 6

GRILLED VEGETABLES

Chop or slice your favorite vegetables into bite-size pieces.
J.W. and Zee usually use:

Onions
Red and/or green peppers
Portobello mushrooms
Eggplant
Summer squash and/or zucchini
and
Odds and ends of veggies that are in the fridge

Parboil such veggies as carrots and broccoli. Marinate
vegetables for $1/2$ hour, adding mushrooms and eggplant
during last few minutes. J.W. and Zee use a marinade
consisting of Good Seasons Garlic and Herb Salad Dressing
made with balsamic vinegar and olive oil. Mesquite-flavored
marinade is also very good.

Place vegetables in a grilling wok (available in your hardware
store) and grill over medium-high heat for 10 minutes,
turning regularly.

Serves 4

*Even people who don't
like vegetables like them
when they're cooked like
this. I often prepare
them this way on a hot
day when it seems best
to cook all of the evening
meal outside on the grill.
Your garden harvest will
never taste better. The
recipe was printed at
the back of* Vineyard
Shadows.

—Shirley

ZUCCHINI SOUTHWESTERN STYLE

Zee was once so overwhelmed by her zucchini crop that she threatened to write an all-zucchini cookbook entitled Zooked until You Glow! *If some unwilling recipient of your excess zucchini crop says, "Take this zucchini and stuff it!" you can enjoy the experience by using this recipe and the next one.*

—Shirley

6 medium zucchini
12 oz. whole kernel corn, frozen or canned
2 eggs, beaten
1/4 cup chopped chives
2 tsp. seasoned salt
1/2 cup grated sharp Cheddar cheese
Paprika

In large saucepan, cook zucchini in boiling water to cover for 5 minutes. Cut zucchini in half lengthwise and remove pulp. Chop pulp and combine with corn, eggs, chives, and salt. Spoon mixture into zucchini shells. Place in 2-qt. oblong baking dish and sprinkle with cheese and paprika. Bake, uncovered, in preheated 350° oven for 30 minutes or until cheese melts.

Serves 6

ZUCCHINI WITH MUSHROOM/ALMOND STUFFING

4 zucchini (7–8" long)
2 tbsp. butter, melted; plus a little extra for the last step
2 scallions, minced
1 cup finely chopped mushrooms
1 clove garlic, crushed
Chopped zucchini flesh

¹/₃ cup grated Swiss cheese

¹/₂ cup almonds, ground in blender

¹/₂ cup dry bread crumbs

¹/₄ tsp. ground cloves

Salt and pepper to taste

1 egg

¹/₂ cup sour cream

¹/₄ cup bread crumbs

¹/₄ cup grated Swiss cheese

Cook zucchini in boiling water to cover for 5 minutes. Cut zucchini in half, lengthwise, remove pulp from shells, and chop zucchini.

Sauté scallions over low heat in 2 tbsp. melted butter, covered, about 5 minutes. Uncover, raise heat to medium, and add next 3 ingredients. Sauté 2–3 minutes longer. Add to chopped zucchini.

Combine next 5 ingredients and add to zucchini mixture.

Whisk egg and sour cream together and add to above mixture. Mixture should be thick enough to mound (add more bread crumbs if necessary).

Spoon mixture into zucchini shells that have been placed in a well-buttered shallow baking dish. Mix remaining bread crumbs and grated cheese together and sprinkle over tops. Drizzle with more melted butter and bake in preheated 400° oven for 20–25 minutes.

Serves 8

Another excellent zucchini dish. There are a lot of them (thank goodness).

—J.W.

GREEN BEANS WITH SHALLOT BUTTER

¹/₂ cup butter or oleo
1 tbsp. olive oil
²/₃ cup thinly sliced shallots
¹/₂ tsp. each salt and pepper
3 lbs. green beans, trimmed
¹/₃ cup fresh parsley (chopped)
Toasted, slivered almonds

The Jacksons and the Craigs grow two or three crops of green beans each season, so they can eat them all summer. This is one of their favorite ways to prepare them. Another excellent way to serve freshly cooked green beans is to drizzle a little Balsamic vinaigrette, or other favorite oil- and vinegar-based dressing, over them while they're still hot. Toss and serve immediately.

—Shirley

Heat 4 tbsp. butter and oil in small skillet until butter melts. Add shallots and cook over low heat 7–9 minutes, stirring occasionally, until tender. Stir in remaining butter, salt, and pepper. Remove from heat.

Cook beans, uncovered, in large pot of boiling water, 5–7 minutes until crisp tender. Drain and transfer to serving bowl.

Add shallot butter and parsley. Toss to coat all and sprinkle with toasted almonds. Serve hot.

Serves 10–12

SWEET POTATO CASSEROLE WITH PRALINE TOPPING

Potato mixture:

3 large eggs

5 lbs. sweet potatoes or yams, boiled, drained, peeled, and mashed (about 6 cups)

$^2/_3$ cup granulated sugar

$^2/_3$ cup unsalted butter, melted

$^1/_3$ cup heavy cream

1 tsp. vanilla

$^1/_2$ tsp. each ground nutmeg and allspice

Topping:

1 cup packed light-brown sugar

$^1/_3$ cup flour

1 cup finely chopped pecans

$^1/_3$ cup unsalted butter, cut in small pieces

Garnish:

12 or more pecan halves

Heat oven to 350°.

Potato mixture: Beat eggs in a large bowl. Stir in potatoes until well blended. Add remaining ingredients and mix well. Spread evenly in greased 2-qt. baking dish.

Topping: Mix sugar, flour, and nuts in medium bowl. Work in butter until well blended. Sprinkle evenly over potato mixture. (If you decide not to use all of topping mix, the remainder may be frozen for future use.)

Bake 60–70 minutes until topping is browned and bubbling. Garnish with pecan halves before serving.

Serves 12

This is good enough to be served as dessert, and always accompanies the Thanksgiving turkey at the Jackson house. It is a sinfully rich dish. Even the kids will love it, and your guests will want the recipe.

—Zee

JOANIE'S POTATO CASSEROLE

1 large bag (24 oz.) frozen hash-brown potatoes
1 pint dairy sour cream
1 bunch scallions, chopped
1 can cream of mushroom soup (undiluted)
2 cups shredded Cheddar cheese (preferably white)
$^{1}/_{2}$ cup French-fried onion rings, crushed
4 tbsp. unsalted butter, melted

My good friend Joanie Cosselman used to contribute this delicious concoction to "Fat Friday" offerings at the middle school where we both taught. The dish always went home without a speck left in it. It is a great potluck item and serves a gang.

—Shirley

Defrost hash browns. Mix first 5 ingredients together and divide between two 2-qt. baking dishes. Sprinkle crushed onion rings over mixture and drizzle butter over all. Bake at 350°, uncovered, for 35 minutes.

Note: Chopped ham or smoked sausage, such as kielbasa, may be added to potato mixture.

"What I say is that, if a man really likes potatoes, he must be a pretty decent sort of fellow."
—A. A. MILNE

MASHED POTATOES WITH GARLIC

3 lbs. baking potatoes
4 whole cloves garlic, peeled
³/₄ cup half-and-half
¹/₄ cup butter
1¹/₄ tsp. salt
¹/₄ tsp. black pepper
¹/₄ tsp. ground nutmeg (freshly ground is best)

Peel potatoes, cut into 1″ chunks and place, with garlic, in large pot with enough water to cover. Cover pot and bring to a boil. Reduce heat and simmer for 15 minutes or until potatoes are fork-tender. Drain potatoes and garlic in colander and transfer to large bowl.

Add the half-and-half, butter, salt, pepper, and nutmeg. Mash potatoes, crushing garlic into them until evenly mixed throughout.

Serve immediately or let cool and freeze in sealed bag or container. To heat, gently heat potatoes in saucepan, stirring in a little (about ¹/₄ cup) additional half-and-half, if necessary, to achieve desired consistency.

Serves 8

Do you know a man who ever gets enough mashed potatoes? This dish is another one regularly served at the Craigs' Thanksgiving meal. It can be prepared ahead of that busy day.

—Shirley

ALIGOT (Potato Puree)

2 lbs. old potatoes
2 tbsp. heavy cream
$1/4$ tsp. salt
$1/8$ tsp. pepper
2 tbsp. unsalted butter
2 large cloves garlic, minced
6 oz. Brie or Camembert, rind removed, sliced
Chopped chives

Now just look at this ingredient list. How could such a concoction be anything other than absolutely delish?

—J.W.

Cook potatoes, in boiling salted water to cover, for 20 minutes or until tender. Drain, peel, and mash with heavy cream. Season with salt and pepper.

Melt butter in small saucepan. Sauté garlic in butter for 1 minute. Add Brie and stir until completely melted.

Stir melted cheese mixture into mashed potatoes and garnish with chopped chives. Serve immediately.

Makes 6 servings

CORN CASSEROLE WITH
JALAPENO PEPPERS AND CHEESE

2 16-oz. cans white corn or yellow corn, drained
1 8-oz. container of cream cheese with chives and onion
3–4 fresh jalapeno peppers, seeded and chopped, or 1 4-oz.
can chopped jalapeno peppers

Combine ingredients in 1^1/$_2$-quart covered casserole and
bake, covered, in 350° oven for about 30 minutes or until
heated through.

Serves 8

*This is my kind of food:
simple and good, with a
taste of Mexico.*

—J.W.

Sauces and Salsas

"I MADE A BATCH OF MY SPAGHETTI
SAUCE, OF WHICH THERE IS NONE
BETTER, THE SECRET INGREDIENTS
BEING A CAN OF CREAM OF
MUSHROOM SOUP AND A GOOD
SHOT OF DONA FLORA'S
BEAN SUPREME, WHICH,
LIKE ONIONS, IMPROVES ALMOST
ANY DISH THAT ISN'T DESSERT."

—J.W., IN *VINEYARD SHADOWS*

MOCK HOLLANDAISE SAUCE

A quick and easy way to make something special. Try it over poached eggs as in Eggs Benedict or over Crab Toasts with Asparagus, or to dress plain asparagus.

—Zee

¹/₄ cup dairy sour cream
¹/₄ cup good mayonnaise
1 scant tsp. lemon juice
Dash bottled hot pepper sauce

Combine all ingredients. Cook and stir over low heat until heated through. Do not boil.

Makes about ¹/₂ cup sauce

MUSHROOM AND LEEK SAUCE

Another "can't go wrong" combination. Surely you can come up with several ways to use this sauce. Try it served over Chicken Cutlets (see page 113).

—Shirley

8 oz. sliced mushrooms
4 medium leeks, sliced thinly
1 cup milk or half-and-half
1 tsp. flour
Salt and pepper to taste

Sauté mushrooms and leeks in butter or oil. Season with salt and pepper. Stir over medium heat for 1–2 minutes. Sprinkle with flour and stir. Add milk. Reduce heat, cover, and cook for 2–3 minutes.

PEANUT DIPPING SAUCE

1 large onion (cut into chunks)
2 cloves garlic
1 tbsp. water
3 tbsp. salad oil
$1/4$ tsp. ground red pepper (cayenne)
1 tsp. coriander
2 tbsp. brown sugar
2 tbsp. lemon juice
2 tbsp. soy sauce
$1/4$ cup peanut butter
$3/4$ cup milk

Combine first 3 ingredients in food processor or blender and whirl until smooth. Heat oil in small pan. Add onion mixture and cook until very soft. Stir in remaining ingredients. Remove from heat and gradually stir in $3/4$ cup milk. Cook over low heat, stirring constantly, until heated through.

With only a little effort you can produce a sauce that's much better than the bottled varieties. It is excellent served with pork or chicken saté or as a dipping sauce for leftover cooked chicken tenders or chicken nuggets.

—Phil

J.W.'S SPAGHETTI SAUCE

J.W. cooks spaghetti and meatballs in Off Season. *Most of the time he uses this sauce, which he and I modestly consider the world's best. I usually keep a batch in the freezer for an impromptu supper. The recipe appears in* Murder at a Vineyard Mansion.

—Phil

2–3 tbsp. cooking oil
1 large onion, chopped
1/2 red or green sweet pepper, chopped
8 oz. sliced mushrooms
2 cloves garlic, chopped (or you can use the chopped garlic in oil that you can buy in the grocery store. It's quite satisfactory and a lot more convenient.)
1 lb. ground meat (You can use ground turkey or chicken if you don't eat mammals.)
1 lb. hot sausages (or spicy Italian-style turkey sausages, if you prefer), sliced
1 small can (5 oz.) of tomato paste
1 can cream of mushroom soup (the secret ingredient!)
1 cup or so of red wine
2 tbsp., more or less, dried parsley
2 tbsp., more or less, dried oregano
1 tsp., more or less, dried rosemary
1 tsp., more or less, dried sage
1 tsp., more or less, dried thyme
1 tsp. or more Dona Flora's Bean Supreme*
Salt and pepper to taste

In a large frying pan, sauté onion, sweet pepper, mushrooms, garlic, and meat. Mix together in frying pan, if cooked separately. Add remaining ingredients and mix thoroughly. Cook over low heat for 20 minutes.

Serve, topped with grated Parmesan cheese, over the pasta of your choice. J.W.'s choice is vermicelli. The sauce can be frozen and used later.

This recipe may, of course, be altered according to your tastes. If you prefer other spices, for instance, use them instead of these. Feel free, too, to change proportions of ingredients.

*Bean Supreme is a combination of spices available from Dona Flora, P.O. Box 77, LaConner, WA 98257. It's also wonderful in any hot bean dish, such as chili or red beans and rice.

MUSTARD CREAM SAUCE

$^1/_4$ cup dry white wine
$^1/_2$ cup heavy cream
1 tsp. Dijon mustard
3 tbsp. unsalted butter

In medium skillet, bring wine, cream, and mustard to a boil. Continue to cook, stirring constantly, until reduced by half. Stir in butter until melted. Keep warm until serving time.

This recipe makes enough sauce to serve over 1$^1/_2$ lbs. of asparagus spears and can be substituted for Hollandaise Sauce in many recipes.

—Shirley

MAKE-AHEAD GRAVY

$1/2$ cup minced onion

1 clove garlic, minced

2 cups chicken broth

3 tbsp. flour

$1/4$ cup apple juice

1 tbsp. lemon juice

$1/2$ cup evaporated milk (may be skim)

1 tsp. Gravy Master

1 tsp. fresh rosemary leaves, minced, or $1/2$ tsp. dried leaves

$1/4$ tsp. dried thyme leaves, crushed

Salt and pepper to taste

3 tbsp. drippings from roasted turkey or chicken

This excellent gravy is typically part of a dinner featuring a roast turkey or chicken. Most of the work can be done a day in advance.

—Phil

In medium saucepan, sauté onion and garlic in 3 tbsp. chicken broth over medium heat for 4 minutes. Add flour and stir 1 minute. Slowly add remaining broth, stirring constantly. Add fruit juices, evaporated milk, Gravy Master, and seasonings. Bring to boil, reduce heat, and simmer for 10 minutes, or until slightly thickened. Remove from heat and process in blender by pulsing for 30 seconds. This portion of recipe may be made a day before needed and refrigerated in a covered container.

30 minutes before ready to serve, place gravy in saucepan over low heat. Whisk in the turkey (or chicken) drippings and simmer on low, stirring occasionally until ready to serve.

Makes 2 cups gravy

DILL SAUCE

Equal portions of mayonnaise and your favorite mustard
Dried dill to taste

Mix these ingredients, making as much as you need, and cover the top of a fish fillet before cooking.

This simple sauce is very good with fish. Try it on salmon, swordfish, or bluefish. Sprinkle a few capers over the fillets before serving.

—Phil

TARTAR SAUCE

$^1/_2$ cup mayonnaise minus 1 tbsp.
$^1/_4$ cup well-drained sweet relish
1 tbsp. finely minced sweet Spanish onion
Some capers, finely chopped (if you have them on hand)

Mix all ingredients together.

Makes $^3/_4$ cup

A no-brainer, but it's reassuring to know that you probably have the ingredients on hand. This sauce is typically served with fried clams, calamari, or fried fish.

—J.W.

MADEIRA GRAVY

1 onion, coarsely chopped
2 large carrots, peeled and chopped
1 stalk celery, chopped
1 tbsp. olive oil
3 cups chicken broth
Drippings from roasted turkey or chicken
$1/2$ cup Madeira
$1^1/2$ tbsp. cornstarch
$1/4$ tsp. salt
$1/4$ tsp. pepper

A gravy that is typically served at a dinner featuring roast turkey or chicken. Part of the work can be done ahead, and the Madeira adds a nice touch.

—J.W.

Sauté onion, carrots, and celery in oil for 15 minutes. (Giblets may be sautéed with vegetables if desired.)

Add broth and simmer for 15 minutes. Strain liquid into bowl and discard solids. (You may chop giblets to add to gravy if desired.) This liquid may be refrigerated for up to 8 hours if you want to make it ahead.

Strain pan drippings into bowl and chill (or freeze) to solidify fat. Skim fat from chilled drippings.

Add Madeira to roasting pan and boil for 1 minute over medium heat, scraping bottom. Strain into saucepan. Add drippings and broth to saucepan and bring to a simmer.

Dissolve cornstarch in 2 tbsp. cold water. Whisk into broth and simmer, whisking until slightly thickened (about 2 minutes). Add salt and pepper (and chopped giblets, if using).

Makes about 3 cups

CUMBERLAND SAUCE

$^{1}/_{2}$ cup port
1 cup orange juice
$^{1}/_{2}$ cup lemon juice
1 cup red currant jelly
$^{1}/_{2}$ cup chopped onion
1 tsp. dry mustard
$^{1}/_{4}$ tsp. ground ginger
A few drops of hot pepper sauce
$1^{1}/_{2}$ tbsp. arrowroot powder (or cornstarch, which makes a less transparent sauce)
1 tbsp. coarsely shredded orange peel
1 tbsp. coarsely shredded lemon peel

Combine first 8 ingredients in a saucepan and bring to a boil, stirring occasionally (mixture may foam up a bit). Strain the sauce.

Combine arrowroot with a little of the sauce in a small bowl and mix well. Stir this into the rest of the sauce and cook over low heat, stirring constantly, until slightly thickened. Do not allow to boil.

Add orange and lemon peel. Serve hot.

This sauce is traditionally served with wild game or birds. The citrus flavor complements even domestic duck or goose.

—Zee

CLASSIC PESTO

1 1/2 cups fresh basil leaves (packed)
2 cloves garlic
1/4 cup pine nuts
1/2–3/4 cup freshly grated Parmesan cheese
1/2–3/4 cup olive oil

Process basil leaves in food processor by pulsing until finely chopped. Do not overprocess or leaves will turn brown. Add pine nuts and garlic and process until mixed. Add grated cheese, using enough to make a thick mixture when processed. With processor running, slowly drizzle in olive oil until desired consistency is achieved (usually that of creamed butter).

Our garden always includes lots of basil, most of which goes into the making of pesto, which we use in all sorts of delicious ways.

—Shirley

Pesto may be spooned into small jars. Pour a thin film of olive oil over top to seal out air, cover tightly, and refrigerate. Sealed jars of pesto may be frozen for even longer storage.

This savory concoction is delicious served over pasta or baked potatoes, spread on bread when making chicken sandwiches, used to flavor dipping oils or added to soups and stews. You'll probably find many more reasons to indulge.

Makes 2 cups

CILANTRO PESTO

2 cups cilantro leaves
4 cloves garlic (equivalent amount of minced garlic in a jar is acceptable)
$^1/_4$ cup pine nuts
$^1/_4$ cup freshly grated Parmesan cheese
$^1/_2$ cup extra-virgin olive oil

Process cilantro, garlic, and nuts in a food processor to a thick puree. Add cheese and pulse to blend. Slowly add enough olive oil to make a thick paste. If not using immediately, transfer mixture to a lidded glass container and cover with a thin layer of olive oil. Refrigerate or freeze for future use.

Makes 1 cup

This is an interesting variation of the classic pesto made with basil. It makes a good addition to Mexican cuisine or you can try it, thinned with cream, as a sauce to accompany steamed mussels.

—Zee

Mayonnaise: One of the sauces which serve the French in place of a state religion.
—Ambrose Bierce

MANGO-CUCUMBER-GREEN ONION SALSA

1 cup chopped ripe fruit (mangos, nectarines, pears, peaches, or plums)
1 cup chopped, seeded cucumber
2 tbsp. thinly sliced green onion
1 tbsp. sugar
1 tbsp. salad oil
1 tbsp. vinegar (preferably balsamic)

Combine all ingredients and mix well. Chill 1–2 hours, or as long as overnight.

A good accompaniment to shrimp, salmon, or chicken entrées, or to Indonesian saté, Indian curry dishes, or Spanish paella. We like mangos, but you can use any of several fruits.

—Shirley

CRANBERRY-ORANGE RELISH WITH GINGER

1 whole seedless, navel orange and the juice of 1 orange
1 cup sugar
1 tbsp. crystallized ginger, chopped finely
12 oz. raw cranberries
Red pepper flakes, optional

Dice oranges into fine pieces—peel, pulp, and all. Place in saucepan with juice, sugar, and ginger, and cook slowly until orange pieces are translucent and liquid thickens to syrup consistency (about 20 minutes). Add cranberries and simmer until they burst, stirring frequently. Season with pepper flakes if desired.

Serve warm or cold.

Excellent served with Thanksgiving turkey.

Freezes well.

We serve this relish at Thanksgiving. It's delicious and adds a festive dash of color to the holiday table.

—Phil

FRIED SAGE LEAVES

Wash 2–3 dozen fresh sage leaves and pat dry with paper towels. Allow to dry completely before proceeding.

Batter:
2 eggs
1/4 tsp. salt
1 cup water
1 1/4 cups flour
Peanut oil

A Tuscan specialty, these may be prepared with or without a batter. The battered variety makes a unique hors d'oeuvre and can really perk up grilled chicken or even burgers.

—Shirley

Beat eggs with salt, and pour in water and the flour. Mix well, breaking up any lumps with a fork.

Heat peanut oil, 2″ deep, in heavy skillet to 350°. Dip sage leaves in batter and drop in hot oil. Deep fry for about 2 minutes or until leaves are crisp. Drain on paper towels and keep warm in oven while frying remaining leaves. Serve immediately, if possible.

Sage leaves may be fried without the batter, in much the same manner, and are a tasty accompaniment to hamburgers cooked on the grill. Try it!

Preserves and Pickles

"LATER IN THE SUMMER I WOULD PICK
THE BEACH PLUMS I'D USE TO MAKE
THE MANY JARS OF JELLY I WOULD
THEN SELL AT OUTRAGEOUS
PRICES. . . . MY BEACH PLUM
PICKING PLACE IS ONE OF
MY MOST CLOSELY GUARDED
SECRETS, ONE I SHARE
WILLINGLY ONLY WITH ZEE."

—J.W., IN *DEATH ON A VINEYARD BEACH*

BREAD-AND-BUTTER PICKLES

4 qts. thinly sliced cucumbers

$1/2$ cup pickling salt (or $1/2$ cup plus 2 tbsp. kosher salt)

Ice cubes

1 tbsp. celery seeds

2 tbsp. mustard seeds

1 tbsp. ground ginger

1 tsp. ground turmeric

$1/2$ tsp. white pepper

4 cups granulated sugar

1 qt. white vinegar

2 qts. thinly sliced onions

J.W. and Zee grow pickling cucumbers in their garden, and any extras are preserved in this popular way. Almost any sandwich is enhanced by a stash of bread-and-butter pickles!
—Shirley

Place sliced cucumbers in large bowl. Gently stir salt into cucumbers. Cover with ice cubes and let stand for 2-3 hours, until cucumbers are crisp and cold. Add ice as needed. Drain cucumbers, rinse well, and add onions. Set aside.

Combine remaining ingredients, except onions, in non-reactive kettle and bring quickly to a boil. Boil for 10 minutes.

Add cucumber/onion mixture to kettle and bring back to boiling point. Pack at once into hot, sterilized jars. Seal and process in boiling water bath for 10-15 minutes.

Remove jars from canner, complete seal, and cool on wire racks.

Makes 5-6 pints

ZUCCHINI DILL PICKLES

3 qts. zucchini, cut lengthwise into strips which will fit into
canning jars
6 cloves garlic
1/4 cup pickling salt
2 1/2 cups white vinegar
2 1/2 cups water
3 sprigs fresh dill
3 grape leaves
18 peppercorns

Combine garlic, salt, vinegar, and water. Bring to a rolling
boil. Place 2 garlic cloves in each hot, sterilized jar. Arrange
zucchini sticks upright in jars; add dill and peppercorns
and top with grape leaves. Pour in hot pickling juice. Seal
and process in a boiling water bath for 10 minutes.

Makes 3 quarts

*Still need another way
to use the remainder of
that zucchini crop? Try
this alternative to
cucumber dill pickles.*

—Zee

*Summer in a jar: The Jacksons and
the Craigs make most of these preserves
and pickles from what they grow in their
garden and find growing wild.*

GRAPE CHUTNEY SAUCE

5 lbs. ripe concord grapes (6–8 cups pulp)
3 lbs. granulated sugar
1 pint cider vinegar
1 tbsp. ground cinnamon
1 tbsp. ground allspice
1 tbsp. ground cloves
$1/2$ tsp. salt
1 tbsp. ground black pepper

This is a very old recipe sometimes referred to as "grape ketsup." It is excellent served with wild game, pork, added to meatloaf, or in place of chutney or sweet and sour sauce. You'll find that it's a very versatile and tasty condiment.

—Shirley

Wash and stem grapes, put in blender, in batches, and chop for 30 seconds. Put through vegetable mill to strain out seeds. Discard seeds. Add remaining ingredients to grape pulp, bring to boiling point in large stainless steel or enameled kettle and simmer until desired consistency (about 1–1$1/2$ hours in wide-mouth kettle).

When desired consistency is reached (test by putting a small amount on a saucer and allowing to cool), pour into hot, sterilized jars and seal.

Makes about 4 pints

APRICOT CHUTNEY

3 large, sweet red peppers, diced
12 oz. dried apricots, diced
1 cup golden raisins
1 cup sugar
1 large onion, finely chopped
$^3/_4$ cup red wine vinegar (may substitute cider vinegar)
5 garlic cloves, minced
$1^1/_2$ tsp. salt
$1^1/_2$ tsp. crushed red pepper flakes
$^1/_4$ tsp. ground ginger
$^1/_4$ tsp. ground cumin
$^1/_4$ tsp. dry mustard

In a large, heavy saucepan, combine all ingredients and bring to a boil. Reduce heat and simmer, uncovered, for 25–30 minutes or until thickened, stirring occasionally.

Ladle into hot, sterilized $^1/_2$-pint jars, clean rims, and seal with two-part lids.

Makes about 4 cups

Chutney can be made from a variety of fruits, and this is one of our favorites. It can be served alongside of poultry or game entrées, or spooned over a block of cream cheese and served as an appetizer to be spread on crackers.

—Phil and Shirley

BEACH PLUM JELLY

3$\frac{1}{2}$ cups juice (from about 2 qts. ripe beach plums)

6 cups sugar

1 (3-oz.) pouch liquid pectin

$\frac{1}{2}$ tsp. butter

This jelly is also known as "summer in a jar." To pick the plums, the Jacksons and Craigs brave the August heat and the rampant poison ivy that always seems to thrive where the juiciest plums grow. Shirley and Zee make the jelly, and what they don't give away or keep for their families, they sell at a local farm stand. It makes a great gift for off-island houseguests. This jelly won a Blue Ribbon at the Topsfield Fair.

—Phil

To prepare juice:

In large stainless steel or enameled pot, thoroughly crush about 2 quarts of beach plums with a potato masher. Add 2$\frac{1}{2}$ cups water and bring to a boil. Simmer, covered, for 30 minutes. Place in jelly bag or several thicknesses of cheesecloth and hang to drip over a large pot. You may squeeze the bag, but the jelly will not be as clear as when allowed to drip.

Measure 3$\frac{1}{2}$ cups of juice into large, nonreactive pot. Add the sugar and butter and mix well.

Place over high heat and bring to a boil, stirring constantly. At once, stir in liquid pectin and bring to a full rolling boil (one which cannot be stirred down). Boil hard for 1 minute, stirring constantly. Remove from heat, skim off any foam with a metal spoon, and pour quickly into hot, sterilized jars. Clean rims of jars and cover with two-piece lids or paraffin.

Makes about 8 half-pint jars of jelly

BLUEBARB JAM

1¹/₂ cups prepared rhubarb (about 1 lb. fresh)
4 cups blueberries (mashed)
6¹/₂ cups sugar
1 (3-oz.) pouch liquid pectin
¹/₄ cup water
¹/₂ tsp. butter

Thinly slice (or chop) rhubarb. Do not peel. Simmer, in nonreactive pot, in ¹/₄ cup water, covered, until soft (1–2 minutes). Crush blueberries with a potato masher and combine with rhubarb. Measure 3¹/₂ cups combined fruit into large stainless steel or enameled saucepan and add sugar and butter. Mix well.

Place over high heat, bring to a full rolling boil, and boil hard for 1 minute, stirring constantly. Remove from heat and stir in liquid pectin at once. Skim off any foam with a metal spoon, and stir a bit to prevent floating fruit. Ladle into hot, sterilized jars; wipe rims, and seal with two-piece lids or paraffin.

Makes about 8 half-pint jars of jam

This jam was born in Shirley's kitchen and was a best seller at the West Tisbury Farmers' Market. The recipe may be found in the back of A Fatal Vineyard Season.

—Phil

SPICED PEACH JAM

4 cups prepared fruit (peeled and pitted peaches, ground or finely chopped)
$1/4$ cup lemon juice
$7^1/2$ cups sugar
1 (3 oz.) pouch liquid pectin
1 tsp. whole cloves
$1/2$ tsp. whole allspice
1 stick cinnamon

Its golden color will remind you of a summer's day even in the dead of winter.

Try it in a peanut butter and jelly sandwich instead of the usual grape jelly.

—Shirley

Combine fruit with lemon juice in large nonreactive pot. Tie spices in cheesecloth bag and add to pot. Simmer fruit with spices for 10 minutes. Add sugar and bring to a full, rolling boil over high heat. Remove spice bag. Boil hard for 1 minute, stirring constantly.

Remove from heat and stir in pectin at once. Skim off foam with large metal spoon if necessary. Ladle into hot, sterilized $1/2$-pt. jars, leaving $1/4''$ head space. Seal immediately. Invert jars for 5 minutes to prevent floating fruit, then turn right-side-up to cool.

Makes 8–9 $1/2$-pt. jars

HOT PEPPER JELLY

$^1/_2$ cup seeded and chopped hot peppers (use jalapenos for
green jelly or red chilis for red jelly)
$^3/_4$ cup seeded and chopped sweet peppers (green or red to
match hot pepper color)
1 cup white or cider vinegar
$^1/_2$ cup cider vinegar
6 cups sugar
$^1/_2$ tsp. unsalted butter
6–7 drops green food coloring for green jelly (optional)
4 drops red food coloring for red jelly (optional)
1 (3 oz.) pouch liquid pectin

Place first 3 ingredients in blender and blend at high speed.
Pour into nonreactive kettle and add the remaining $^1/_2$ cup
of vinegar, the sugar, butter, and food coloring, if using.
Bring to rolling boil, stirring constantly. Add 3 oz. liquid
pectin, stir and boil 1 minute.

Remove from heat, skim any foam, and stir to distribute
particles evenly. Pour into hot, sterilized jars and seal. It is
not necessary to refrigerate after opening.

Serve over a block of cream cheese as an appetizer.

Note: One jar each of red and green jelly makes a nice
Christmas or hostess gift.

*I don't eat many jellies,
but this one gets my
attention every time.
I usually eat it with
cream cheese on crackers
as an appetizer. It's both
tasty and colorful.*

—Phil

ONION PICKLES

4 qts. tiny pickling onions, peeled

1 cup salt (non-iodized)

2 cups sugar

$1/4$ cup mustard seed

$2^1/2$ tbsp. prepared horseradish

2 qts. white vinegar

7 bay leaves

7 small red hot peppers (or jalapeno peppers)

These are delicious and were first-prize winners in the Dukes County Fair. Serve them with your next cold buffet.

—Shirley

Cover onions with boiling water and let stand 2 minutes. Drain and put onions in bowl of cold water. Enlist everyone you can to help you peel the onions. This is a bit time-consuming, but fresh onions definitely make the best pickles.

Sprinkle onions with salt, add cold water to cover, and let stand for 12–18 hours in a cool place. Drain, rinse well, and drain again.

Combine sugar, mustard seed, horseradish, and vinegar; simmer 15 minutes. Pack onions into hot, sterilized pint (or 12-oz.) jars, leaving $1/4''$ head space, inserting 1 pepper and 1 bay leaf into each jar. Heat pickling liquid to boiling and pour over onions, leaving $1/4''$ head space. Clean rims of jars and cover with two-piece lids. Process 10 minutes in boiling water bath.

Yields 7 pints

Breads and Muffins

"YOU ALWAYS EAT AT LEAST A HALF
LOAF OF FRESH BREAD AS SOON AS
IT COMES OUT OF THE OVEN."

—J.W. IN *VINEYARD FEAR*

(ISSUED FIRST AS *CLIFF HANGER*)

WHITE BREAD

2 pkgs. active dry yeast
1 cup warm (110–115°) water
3½ cups lukewarm milk (scalded, then cooled)
14–14½ cups unbleached all purpose flour
6 tbsp. sugar
2 tbsp. salt
¼ cup soft shortening

This is the bread that launched Phil's cooking career. An end slice of this bread, hot out of the oven and slathered with butter, is as close as you can come to eating in heaven.

—Shirley

Dissolve the yeast in ½ cup of the warm water. Pour remaining water into large bowl, and stir in sugar and salt until dissolved. Mix in shortening and yeast. Add flour, one half at a time, mixing by hand. When flour is incorporated and mixture leaves sides of bowl, turn out onto floured board and knead until smooth and elastic (about 6–10 minutes). Place dough in greased bowl (turning once so that greased side is up); cover with warm, damp cloth; and let rise in warm, draft-free place until double in bulk (about 1½ hours). Punch down dough, pull edges to center, and turn over in bowl. Let rise again (covered) until almost double (30–45 minutes). Divide dough into 4 parts and let stand, covered, for 10 minutes.

Shape dough into loaves and place in greased 9x5x2″ loaf pans. Let rise again, covered, until dough reaches top of the pan (about 1 hour). Bake in preheated 425° oven for 25–30 minutes or until browned and loaf sounds hollow when tipped out of pan and tapped on the bottom. Cool on wire racks. For a soft-tender crust, brush tops of loaves with butter and cover with towel for a few minutes.

Makes 4 loaves. Eat 1 loaf, slathered with butter, hot out of the oven. Wrap and store (or freeze) the remainder when cool.

DILL YEAST BREAD WITH COTTAGE CHEESE

1 pkg. dry yeast

$^1/_4$ cup warm water

1 cup cottage cheese

2 tbsp. sugar

1 tbsp. minced onion

1 tbsp. unsalted butter, melted

2 tsp. dill seed

1 tsp. salt

$^1/_4$ tsp. baking soda

1 egg

2$^1/_2$ cups flour

Soften yeast in warm water. Warm cottage cheese; then add sugar, onion, butter, dill seed, salt, baking soda, unbeaten egg, and yeast mixture. Add flour to form reasonably stiff dough, beating well. Knead until smooth and elastic.

Cover and let rise in a warm place until light and doubled in size (about 50–60 minutes). Stir dough down and turn into two greased 9x5″ loaf pans (or a greased 8″ round casserole dish). Cover and let rise 30–50 minutes (depending on pan size). Bake in preheated 350° oven for 30–40 minutes (for loaf pans) or 40–50 minutes (for casserole), until golden brown. Turn out onto wire racks and brush with softened butter.

Makes 2 rectangular loaves or 1 larger round loaf

Offer this fragrant loaf with chowder or a fish entrée, or take it to a potluck gathering.

—Phil

MASA SOVADA (Portuguese Sweet Bread)

2 envelopes dry yeast
1 cup sugar*
$^1/_2$ cup warm water (about 115°)
1 tsp. salt
$^1/_2$ cup condensed milk
$^1/_2$ cup room-temperature water
$^1/_2$ cup unsalted butter
4 large eggs
6–7 cups all-purpose flour
$^1/_2$ tsp. vanilla extract
$^1/_2$ tsp. lemon extract
Zest of 1 lemon
$^1/_2$ tsp. ground mace

This bread, which Shirley and Zee learned to bake from their Azorian-descended parents and grandparents, is traditionally served on various feast days, including Easter, at which time whole eggs are sometimes cooked inside the loaves. It is delicious toasted and spread with butter. It freezes well if you can refrain from eating it all up as soon as you cook it.

—Phil

Sprinkle yeast and 1 tsp. sugar into $^1/_2$ cup warm water (about 115°) in a 2-cup measure (it will foam up). Stir until yeast is dissolved; then let stand, undisturbed, to proof, until bubbly and double in volume (about 10 minutes).

Mix condensed milk with the other $^1/_2$ cup of water. Heat $^3/_4$ cup of condensed milk-water mixture with remaining sugar, salt, and butter in a small saucepan, stirring occasionally, until butter is melted. Pour into a large mixing bowl and cool to lukewarm. Add extracts, lemon zest, and mace.

Beat eggs in a small bowl, until frothy. Remove and reserve 2 tbsp. of egg for brushing on loaves.

Add remaining beaten egg, yeast mixture, and 3 cups of flour to milk mixture. Beat with electric mixer until batter is smooth. Add enough of the remaining flour (3–4 cups) to make a soft dough. Too much flour will toughen dough.

Turn dough out onto floured surface. Knead, using additional flour only if necessary, until dough can be handled easily. Continue to knead until dough is smooth and elastic (it will be soft). This step may be done in a free-standing mixer with a dough hook, if you're lucky enough to own such a device.

Press dough into large buttered bowl and turn so that buttered side is up. Cover with buttered plastic wrap and a dishtowel which has been dampened with hot water and wrung out. Let rise, in a warm place, for $1^1/2$ hours or until double in bulk. (I put bowl of dough on upper oven rack with pan of hot water on rack beneath it.)

Punch down dough and turn onto lightly floured surface. Let stand, covered, for 10 minutes. Divide dough in half and shape into two loaves. Place loaves in 2 greased 9x5x3″ loaf pans.

Let rise again in warm place, covered, for about 1 hour, or until double in volume.

Bake in a preheated 350° oven for 35 minutes or until loaves sound hollow when tapped on the bottom. If loaves start to darken too soon, cover loosely with brown paper or aluminum foil. (I cover loaves when just golden, usually after 5–10 minutes.) Remove loaves from pans to cool on wire racks. Brush tops immediately with the reserved beaten egg mixed with about 1 tbsp. water and a little granulated sugar.

Note: This bread may also be shaped into round loaves. Reserve some of the dough (for a lattice top). Press whole raw eggs (shell and all) into top of loaves and cover with ropes of dough, in a latticework fashion, to resemble egg-filled Easter baskets.

* If you prefer a sweeter bread and increase the amount of sugar, the dough will take longer to rise, and you may want to add an additional packet of yeast.

Makes 2 loaves

LOADED (with Grains and Seeds) BREAD

$^1/_2$ cup warm water

2 tsp. granulated yeast (1 packet)

2 tbsp. honey

1 cup all-purpose flour

1 cup whole wheat flour

$^1/_2$ cup buckwheat or rye flour

$^1/_2$ cup soy flour

$^3/_4$ cup roasted sunflower seeds

1 cup whole milk

2 tbsp. butter

1 tsp. salt

Extra flour to achieve kneading consistency

1 egg white

1 recipe Seed Blend (recipe follows)

Zee likes to make this on a cold winter day when it feels good to have the oven on. It goes well with a hearty soup.

—J.W.

Combine water, yeast, and $^1/_2$ tsp. of the honey in a small bowl. Mix.

In a large bowl, combine flours and sunflower seeds.

Heat milk and butter in saucepan until butter melts. Cool until mixture is tepid. Add yeast mixture, salt, and remaining honey. Stir to combine.

Stir milk mixture into flour mixture until blended. Mixture will be sticky.

Add enough extra flour to make dough kneadable.

Turn dough out onto lightly floured board and knead until smooth and elastic. Add only enough flour to keep dough from sticking to board.

Place dough in an oiled bowl (turning ball once so that top is greased), cover with plastic wrap or a dampened towel, and let rise in a warm place for about an hour (until doubled in bulk).

Punch down dough and shape into a round loaf. Place on greased baking sheet (large enough to accommodate raised loaf), cover, and let rise for another hour.

Preheat oven to 350°.

Beat egg white in small bowl until foamy. Brush loaf with the egg white and sprinkle with seed mixture. Gently brush more egg white over seeds.

Bake for 30–35 minutes, until a knife inserted into bottom center of loaf comes out clean.

Makes 1 large loaf

SEED BLEND FOR LOADED BREAD

¹/₄ cup regular oats
2 tbsp. flax seed
2 tbsp. sesame seeds
2 tbsp. pumpkin seeds
2 tbsp. sunflower seeds

Combine all ingredients. Store in an airtight container.

This recipe will make enough seed blend for 2–3 loaves of bread or may be used as a topping for salads, cereals, etc. Toast at 250° for 5 minutes to use as a topping.

WHEAT-GERM HERB BREAD

5–5¹/₂ cups flour

2 pkg. dry yeast

¹/₃ cup sugar

1 tsp. salt

1 tsp. thyme leaves, crushed

1 tsp. marjoram leaves, crushed

¹/₂ cup water

1 cup milk

¹/₂ cup unsalted butter

2 eggs plus 1 egg yolk

1¹/₃ cups wheat germ

1 egg white, beaten

1 tsp. wheat germ

When I had a booth at the West Tisbury Farmers' Market, where the Vineyard's finest gather every Saturday morning in summer, this bread was a favorite among my customers. It also won a blue ribbon at the Topsfield Fair. It makes delicious sandwiches and is good toasted for breakfast.

—Shirley

In large bowl, combine 3 cups flour, yeast, sugar, salt, and herbs; mix well.

In saucepan, heat milk, water, and butter until warm (120–130°), and add to flour mixture. Add eggs and egg yolk. Blend at low speed until moistened, then beat at medium speed for 3 minutes. By hand, gradually stir in 1¹/₃ cups wheat germ and enough remaining flour to make a soft dough. Knead on lightly floured surface until smooth and elastic (about 10 minutes). Place in greased bowl, turning once to grease top. Cover and let rise until light and doubled in bulk (about 1 hour).

Punch down dough and divide into two parts. Roll or pat each part on lightly floured surface to a 12x8″ rectangle. Cut each rectangle into two equal 12″ strips. Pinch ends of each strip together to make a rope. Twist two ropes together, seal ends, and fold under loaf. Place loaves in well-greased 8¹/₂x4¹/₂x2⁵/₈″ (or 9x5″) loaf pans. Cover and let rise again for 30–40 minutes. Lightly brush top with beaten egg white, and sprinkle with the 1 tsp. wheat germ. Bake in a preheated 350° oven for 35–45 minutes. Cover loosely with aluminum foil the last 5–10 minutes of baking. Remove loaves from pans and cool on wire rack.

Makes 2 loaves

IRISH OATMEAL BREAD

3 cups flour
1¼ cups quick oats
1½ tbsp. baking powder
1 tsp. salt
1 egg
¼ cup honey
1½ cups milk
1 tbsp. unsalted butter

Mix dry ingredients together. In separate bowl, beat egg with honey and milk. Pour liquid ingredients into dry ingredients and stir just until all is moistened. Batter will not be smooth.

Spread batter in greased loaf pan and bake in preheated 350° oven for about 1 hour and 15 minutes, or until tester inserted in center comes out clean. Turn loaf out onto wire rack and, while still warm, brush top with butter.

Makes 1 loaf

Shirley and I both have Scottish ancestors, but are more than willing to eat slabs of this fine Irish bread. It goes well with a New England boiled dinner. It also makes a good breakfast topped with Spiced Peach Jam.

—Phil

RAISED MEXICAN CORNBREAD

2 packages dry yeast
1 cup corn meal
1 tbsp. salt
1 tbsp. sugar
$^1/_2$ tsp. baking soda
2 eggs
1 cup buttermilk
$^1/_2$ cup canola oil
1 medium onion, chopped fine
3 canned chili peppers, chopped fine
1 cup cream-style corn
$1^1/_2$ cups Cheddar cheese, grated
5 cups flour
$^1/_4$ cup melted butter

Forget the packaged mix for once, and try this with a bowl of chili or black bean soup. You will be rewarded for your extra effort.

—Shirley

Stir yeast into cornmeal and soda. Heat oil, salt, sugar, onion, and buttermilk to lukewarm. Stir liquid ingredients into dry ingredients. Add eggs and beat thoroughly. Add corn, chopped chili peppers, and cheese. Add flour, 1 cup at a time until well mixed.

Knead dough until smooth and elastic. Grease a large bowl with melted margarine and put dough in bowl, turning once to grease top. Cover and let rise in a warm place until doubled in bulk (about 1–1$^1/_2$ hours).

Grease 3 9x5″ loaf pans and dust lightly with cornmeal. Divide dough into thirds. Roll each third, on a lightly floured surface, into a rectangle, pressing to eliminate air pockets. Fold to fit into pans, placing seam side down. Brush loaves with melted butter, cover, and let rise a second time until double in size.

Bake in preheated 400° oven for 20–30 minutes (until lightly browned and loaves sound hollow when tapped on the bottom). Remove from pans and cool on wire racks, brushing immediately with melted butter to prevent a hard crust. Cool completely.

Makes 3 loaves and freezes very well

CORNBREAD

1 cup yellow cornmeal
1 cup flour
2 tsp. baking powder
$^1/_2$ tsp. baking soda
$^1/_2$ tsp. salt
1 cup buttermilk
1 egg
3 tbsp. sugar
3 tbsp. melted butter

Not quite as tasty as Raised Mexican Cornbread, but easy and delicious. The optional additions make it especially good. Shirl serves it at Thanksgiving.

—Phil

Combine dry ingredients in medium bowl. Combine wet ingredients, separately, and stir into dry ingredients, mixing just enough to thoroughly combine. Let sit a couple of minutes before spreading into greased 8˝ square pan.

Bake in a preheated 350° oven for 20 minutes, or until center is firm.

Optional additions:

1 cup fresh, frozen (defrosted) or canned (drained) corn kernels
$^1/_2$ cup grated mild Cheddar or Jack cheese
Crumbled bacon bits

KIM'S YUMMY CINNAMON ROLLS

4¹/₂–5 cups flour
1 pkg. dry yeast
1 cup milk
¹/₃ cup butter or margarine
¹/₃ cup sugar
3 eggs
¹/₂ tsp. salt

Filling:

³/₄ cup packed light brown sugar
¹/₄ cup flour
1 tbsp. cinnamon
¹/₂ cup unsalted butter
¹/₂ cup chopped pecans
1 tbsp. light cream

Kim Lynch, our daughter, is an excellent cook famed in particular for her chocolate concoctions that have made her a prize winner in almost every one of the chocolate contests in Durango, Colorado. This recipe doesn't contain chocolate, but is, as its name implies, yummy! And you can do most of the preparation the night before.

—Shirley and Phil

In large bowl, mix 2¹/₄ cups flour with the yeast. In small saucepan heat, to about 110°, milk, ¹/₃ cup butter, ¹/₃ cup sugar, and salt just until warm and butter is almost melted. Add to flour mixture. Add eggs and beat on low speed for 30 seconds, scraping sides of bowl. Beat on high speed for 3 minutes. With wooden spoon, beat in as much remaining flour as you can. Knead dough until it is smooth and elastic. Shape into a ball and place in a greased bowl, turning once to grease top. Cover and let rise in a warm place until doubled in bulk (about 1 hour).

For filling:

Combine brown sugar, ¹/₄ cup flour, and cinnamon. Cut in butter until mixture is crumbly. Set aside.

Punch down dough and turn out onto lightly floured surface. Cover and let rise 10 minutes. Roll into a 12″ square.

Sprinkle filling over dough, topping with chopped pecans. Roll up jelly-roll style and pinch edges to seal. Slice in 8–10 1$^1/_2$″ pieces. Arrange dough pieces, cut side up, in a greased baking pan. Cover loosely with plastic wrap, leaving room for rolls to rise. Refrigerate 2–24 hours.

Uncover and let rolls stand at room temperature for 30 minutes. Break surface bubbles with greased toothpick, brush with cream, and bake in preheated 375° oven for 25–30 minutes. Cover with foil the last 10 minutes to prevent over-browning.

Remove rolls from oven and brush again with cream or milk. Carefully invert rolls onto wire rack, cool slightly, and invert onto serving platter. Drizzle with Glaze (recipe follows).

Makes 8–10 rolls

Glaze:

1$^1/_4$ cups confectioner's sugar
1 tsp. light corn syrup
$^1/_2$ tsp. vanilla extract
1–2 tbsp. cream (to make drizzling consistency)

Mix well.

PUMPKIN NUT BREAD

3½ cups flour
2 tsp. baking soda
1½ tsp. salt
1½ tsp. cinnamon
1 tsp. nutmeg
3 cups sugar
1 cup canola oil
4 eggs
⅔ cup water
2 cups mashed pumpkin or squash (freshly cooked or canned)
1 cup chopped pecans or walnuts

This is a nice hostess gift for a harvest-time gathering. It couldn't be easier to make.

—Zee

Preheat oven to 350°. Sift together first 5 ingredients. Add sugar. Make a well in center of dry ingredients and add oil, eggs, water, and pumpkin, all at the same time. Mix well. Add nuts and mix to combine. Pour into 4 ungreased 8x4x2″ loaf pans. Bake for 1 hour or until toothpick comes out clean. Cool on wire rack before removing from pans.

Makes 4 loaves

"A loaf of bread is what we chiefly need.
Pepper and vinegar besides,
are very good indeed."
—THE WALRUS, IN LEWIS CARROLL'S
THE WALRUS AND THE CARPENTER

THE WORLD'S BEST ZUCCHINI BREAD

3 eggs, beaten

2 cups sugar

1 cup canola oil

1 tsp. vanilla extract

1 tsp. cinnamon

1 tsp. salt

1 tsp. baking soda

$1/4$ tsp. baking powder

3 cups flour

2 cups grated zucchini (seed zucchini but do not peel unless squash is large with tough skin)

1 cup chopped nuts (walnuts or pecans)

Mix sugar, oil, and vanilla with beaten eggs. In separate large bowl, combine next 5 ingredients. Stir wet ingredients into dry ingredients just until all is moistened. Fold in grated zucchini and nuts. Turn into two 9x5″ greased loaf pans. Bake at 350° for about 1 hour and 15 minutes or until tester comes out clean. Cool on wire rack before turning out.

Makes 2 loaves (freezes well)

No exaggeration! We inherited this recipe from my mother. This bread is great toasted and spread with cream cheese. Shirley won a blue ribbon with it at the Topsfield Fair. If you're being overrun by your zucchini, you can use up some of it in this delicious way.

—Phil

CRANBERRY-ORANGE NUT BREAD

1½ tsp. baking powder
½ tsp. baking soda
½ tsp. salt
1 cup sugar
2 cups flour (use 1 tbsp. of this to dredge fruit and nuts before adding to batter)
1 cup whole cranberries
1 cup chopped walnuts
2 eggs, beaten
Juice of 1 orange
2 tbsp. melted unsalted butter or oleo
1 tsp. grated orange rind
Hot water

Shirley won blue ribbons for this bread at both the Topsfield Fair in Massachusetts and at the La Plata County Fair in Colorado. Spread it with cream cheese, or toast and butter it while still hot.

—Phil

Mix together first 5 ingredients. In separate bowl, combine eggs, orange juice, melted shortening, and enough hot water (if necessary) to make 1 cup liquid. Stir wet ingredients into dry ingredients, only until mixed. Fold in cranberries and nuts.

Pour into greased 9x5″ loaf pan. Bake at 350° for about 1 hour, or until tester comes out clean. Cool on wire rack for 1 hour before removing from pan.

Note: This recipe will make 3 loaves baked in 6x3⅞″ pans. Bake small loaves for about 40 minutes.

Makes 1 loaf

BEST-EVER BLUEBERRY MUFFINS (Really!)

6 tbsp. unsalted butter
1¼ cups sugar
2 eggs
2 cups flour
½ tsp. salt
2 tsp. baking powder
½ cup milk
1 pint blueberries (don't skimp!)
Cinnamon and sugar mixture (about 2 tbsp.)

Cream butter and sugar together until well blended. Beat in eggs, 1 at a time. In separate bowl, mix flour, salt, and baking powder together. Add, alternately, with milk to egg mixture. Crush ½ cup of the blueberries with a fork, mix into batter, and fold in the remaining blueberries.

Pour into greased muffin tins and sprinkle tops with a mixture of cinnamon and sugar. Bake in a preheated 375° oven for 30 minutes or until tester comes out clean.

Remove muffins from pan, immediately, and cool, on sides, on wire rack.

Makes approximately 12 muffins

A blue ribbon winner. All of the Craigs and Jacksons and their friends love these muffins. You absolutely cannot eat just one.

—Phil

BRAN-FLAKE MUFFINS

5 cups flour
2 tsp. salt
5 tsp. baking soda
2 tsp. cinnamon

Mix above ingredients together in a *very* large bowl.

These bran muffins always sold out instantly the West Tisbury Farmers' Market. One of their charms is that the batter can be kept for weeks and fresh muffins can be made on demand. The recipe— the most asked-for in the series of Phil's Vineyard mysteries—may be found at the back of A Fatal Vineyard Season.

—Shirley

Add:
15 oz. of bran flakes (or Raisin Bran)
2³/₄ cups sugar
1 qt. buttermilk or plain yogurt

Mix well.

Add:
4 beaten eggs
1 cup vegetable oil

Mix well again.

Add:
Grated rind of 3 oranges (about 3 tbsp.) or equivalent amount of chopped crystallized ginger, raisins, etc.
1 cup chopped walnuts or pecans

Mix all ingredients together well. Store in container with a tight lid in refrigerator for up to 6 weeks.

To bake: Do not stir batter. Nearly fill desired number of greased muffin cups. Sprinkle tops with sugar. Bake in preheated 375° oven for about 20 minutes or until pick inserted in center of muffin comes out clean.

FOCACCIA BREAD

Dough:

2 envelopes quick-rising yeast
2 cups warm water (about 110°)
1 tbsp. sugar
4 tbsp. olive oil
$\frac{1}{2}$ cup vegetable (canola) oil
1 tsp. salt
$5\frac{1}{2}$ cups unbleached white flour
Topping mixture (see below)

Dissolve yeast in water. Add sugar, olive oil, canola oil, and salt. Mix in 3 cups of flour and blend until dough leaves sides of mixing bowl (about 10 minutes). Mix in enough of the remaining flour to make a kneadable dough, and knead on lightly floured board until smooth and elastic. Allow the dough to rise, covered, until doubled twice in the bowl, punching down after each rising.

Divide dough between two (18x13″) oiled baking sheets. Press dough out to edges of each pan with your fingers. Allow to rise again for about 30 minutes. Brush with oil and garlic and sprinkle with rosemary and salt (see topping ingredients below), or brush with basil pesto that has been thinned with olive oil.

Bake in preheated 375° oven for about 20 minutes.

Makes 2 loaves

Here's a change from your usual baked bread. It has a Mediterranean air, and goes especially well with Italian, Spanish, and Greek dishes.

—Shirley

Topping for Focaccia Bread:

3 cloves garlic, crushed
$\frac{1}{4}$ cup olive oil
1 tbsp. dried rosemary leaves, chopped
1 tbsp. kosher salt

Desserts

"GOD WAS PROBABLY A BAKER."

—J.W. IN *VINEYARD SHADOWS*

AUNT ELSIE'S PIE CRUST

2 cups flour
Pinch of salt
Pinch of baking powder
1 cup shortening
1/2 cup cold water

Phil and J.W. use this wonderful crust for all of their pies. Phil got it from his Aunt Elsie Kiefer, who made better pies than anyone he knew until he started making his own, which, thanks to the pie crust, he thinks are just as good as hers! J.W., in turn, got the recipe from Phil, and now bows to no one in the best pie competition.

—Shirley

Mix first three ingredients together.

Cut into above mixture: 1 cup shortening (until small granules form)

Mix in 1/2 cup cold water.

This makes a very sticky dough. Use lots of flour when rolling out. Place bottom crust in pie pan and spread with softened butter. Sprinkle with sugar for dessert pies or flour for main dish pies or quiches to keep crust from absorbing juices.

Makes approximately three 8–9″ crusts

JEFF'S APPLE PIE

6 cups sliced Granny Smith–type apples
$^1/_4$ cup packed brown sugar
$^1/_2$–$^3/_4$ cup granulated sugar
2 tbsp. flour
$^1/_4$ tsp. salt
1–1$^1/_2$ tsp. cinnamon
$^1/_2$ tsp. nutmeg
1–2 tbsp. unsalted butter
Sprinkle of lemon juice
Pastry for a 2-crust (9″) pie

J.W. likes a sweet apple pie, so he uses a good amount of sugar and spices in his recipe. Of course, he also uses Aunt Elsie's pie crust!

—Shirley

Preheat oven to 425°. Place bottom crust in pie plate, smear with softened butter and sprinkle with granulated sugar. Fill crust with apple slices. Mix next 6 ingredients together and sprinkle over apples. Dot with small pieces of butter and sprinkle with a little lemon juice. Cover with top crust, seal edges, and slash to allow steam to escape. Top crust may be sprinkled with a mixture of cinnamon and sugar, if desired. Bake about 40–45 minutes, or until crust is golden brown. Serve with vanilla ice cream or slabs of good Cheddar cheese. Jeff prefers the former, Zee the latter.

"No man's pie is freed from his ambitious finger."
—SHAKESPEARE, *HENRY VIII*

BRANDIED PEACH STREUSEL PIE

Pastry for one 9″ pie crust

Streusel topping:
1/2 cup flour
1/3 cup packed light brown sugar
1/4 cup wheat germ
1/4 cup butter, cut in small pieces

Pie filling:
2 1/2 lbs. ripe peaches (about 6 large)
3/4 cup granulated sugar
2 tbsp. flour
1 tbsp. lemon juice
1/4 cup brandy
1/4 stick (1/8 cup) unsalted butter
Confectioner's sugar

Another blue-ribbon winner at the Topsfield Fair. I made up this pie recipe when I discovered that I'd used up all of the recipes I knew in previous Topsfield Fair pie competitions.

—Phil

Combine flour, sugar, and wheat germ for streusel filling and cut in butter. Set aside.

Drop peaches, 3 or 4 at a time, into boiling water. Leave in 15–30 seconds. Then remove to a bowl of cold water. Peel, halve, pit, and slice peaches. You should have about 5 cups.

Mix sugar, 1/4 cup flour, and lemon juice in large bowl. Add peach slices and toss to mix. Sprinkle with brandy and toss lightly. Line bottom of pie plate with pastry, turn under edges, and flute. Smear pastry with softened butter and sprinkle with sugar. Spoon peach mixture into pastry shell and dot with 2 tbsp. of the butter. Cover filling with non-stick or greased aluminum foil.

Bake in 425° oven for 15 minutes, then lower temperature to 350°. Continue baking 30 minutes or until juices bubble up.

Remove foil and sprinkle with streusel topping. Bake 15 minutes longer or until top is set and lightly browned.

Cool on wire rack for at least 1 hour. Dust top with confectioner's sugar. Garnish with additional peach slices if desired.

PECAN PIE

$^1/_2$ cup sugar
$^1/_4$ cup unsalted butter
1 cup light corn syrup
$^1/_4$ tsp. salt
3 eggs
1 cup pecan halves
1 (9") pastry shell

It's probably fair to say that there has never been a bad pecan pie.

—J.W.

J.W. is quite vain about this one.

—Zee

Cream butter and sugar together. Add syrup and salt and beat well. Beat in eggs, 1 at a time. Add pecan halves.

Pour into pastry shell and bake in preheated 350° oven for 50–70 minutes or until knife inserted in center comes out clean. Cover loosely with aluminum foil if pie is browning too fast.

Serve with whipped cream.

PUMPKIN PIE

A Thanksgiving favorite. You can make this pie using the baked and pureed flesh of a real pumpkin, or the canned kind. Some people swear by the former, and there's no question that the texture of the puree is different from what you get from a can. Still, not everyone wants to wrestle with a real pumpkin, and for such cooks the canned puree is fine.

—Shirley

2 eggs, lightly beaten
2 cups pumpkin puree
$^3/_4$ cup sugar
$^1/_2$ tsp. salt
1 tsp. ground cinnamon
$^1/_2$ tsp. ground ginger
$^1/_4$ tsp. ground cloves
1$^2/_3$ cups evaporated milk or light cream
1 (9″) pastry shell, smeared with softened butter and sprinkled with sugar, or coat with beaten egg white, which may act as a better barrier against moisture

Mix first 8 ingredients together and pour into prepared pastry shell. Bake in preheated 425° oven for 15 minutes, then reduce heat to 350° and continue baking for about 45 minutes or until knife inserted into center comes out clean. Cover edges of pastry with aluminum foil if browning too rapidly.

Serve with whipped cream and chopped nuts or with wedges of Cheddar cheese.

BRANDY ALEXANDER PIE

1 envelope unflavored gelatin
1/2 cup cold water
2/3 cup sugar
1/8 tsp. salt
3 eggs, separated
1/4 cup cognac
1/4 cup crème de cocoa
2 cups heavy cream, whipped
10″ chocolate cookie crumb crust (for recipe, see page 222
for Café Mocha Cheesecake)
Shaved chocolate for garnish

Sprinkle gelatin over cold water in saucepan. Add 1/3 cup sugar, salt, and egg yolks. Stir to blend. Place over low heat and keep stirring while gelatin dissolves and mixture thickens. Do not boil. Remove from heat and stir in cognac and crème de cacao. Chill until mixture starts to mound slightly (about 30 minutes).

Beat egg whites stiff, gradually beating in remaining 1/3 cup sugar. Fold into gelatin mixture.

Whip 1 cup cream and fold into mixture. Pour into chocolate crumb crust. Chill several hours or overnight.

When ready to serve, garnish with remaining cup of cream, whipped, and chocolate shaved into curls.

Makes one 10″ pie

This sweet, chocolaty pie requires very little cooking. It's a nice one for summer meals on the porch or in the yard.

—Shirley

KEY LIME PIE

1 (9") pre-baked pastry shell
3 eggs, separated
1 (14-oz.) can sweetened, condensed milk
$^{1}/_{2}$ cup lime juice
A few drops of green food coloring, if desired (go easy on this)
$^{1}/_{2}$ tsp. cream of tartar
$^{1}/_{3}$ cup sugar

This is one of those pies that refreshes you as you eat it, much like chilled vino verde refreshes you as you drink it. You can use a purchased pastry shell or make your own, using Aunt Elsie's Pie Crust.

—Phil

Beat egg yolks in bowl, then stir in condensed milk, lime juice, and coloring (if desired). Pour into pastry shell. In separate bowl, beat egg whites with cream of tartar until soft peaks form. Gradually add sugar, beating until stiff. Spread meringue on pie, being sure to seal to edge of crust. Bake in preheated 350° oven for 12 minutes. Cool, then chill in refrigerator.

Makes one 9" pie

APRICOT SQUARES

²/₃ cup dried apricots (rinse, cover with water, and boil 10 minutes; drain, cool, and chop)
¹/₂ cup soft butter
¹/₄ cup sugar
1 cup flour

Mix butter, sugar, and flour until crumbly and press into greased 8x8″ pan. Bake in preheated 350° oven for 25 minutes.

¹/₃ cup flour
¹/₂ tsp. baking powder
¹/₄ tsp. salt
2 eggs (beaten)
1 cup light brown sugar
¹/₂ tsp. vanilla
¹/₂ cup chopped nuts (pecans or walnuts)
Powdered sugar

Shirley makes these squares and Phil eats them. Zee and J.W. both make them and eat them. Their children eat them. Shirl eats them. Everybody eats them.

—Shirley and Phil

Sift together flour, baking powder, and salt. In separate bowl, add brown sugar to beaten eggs and beat well. Add flour mixture, vanilla, nuts, and chopped apricots to egg mixture, and mix. Spread mixture over baked layer and bake at 350° for 30 minutes. Cool in pan and cut into squares. Coat squares in powdered sugar before serving.

Makes 16–25 squares

LEMON TART WITH BERRIES

Crust:
30 square shortbread cookies (like Lorna Doones)
6 tbsp. unsalted butter, melted
$1/4$ cup confectioners' sugar

Filling:
2 eggs
3 egg yolks
$3/4$ cup sugar
$1/2$ cup fresh lemon juice
1 tbsp. grated lemon rind
$1/2$ cup cold, unsalted butter—cut into pieces

Garnish:
$1/2$ cup heavy cream, whipped
Fresh berries (raspberries, blackberries, strawberries, blueberries, or a combination)
Mint sprigs

This tart makes your taste buds jump up and down and make little moans of delight.

—Shirley

Whirl cookies in food processor until finely crumbed. Add butter and sugar and process until combined. Spread crumbs, pressing evenly, onto bottom and sides of 9″ tart pan with removable bottom. Refrigerate until firm.

Stir eggs, egg yolks, sugar, and lemon juice together in a heavy saucepan. Cook over low heat, stirring constantly, until thickened and just starting to simmer (about 6–10 minutes). Do not stir too vigorously.

Place pan in large bowl of cold water and stir in butter until blended. Cover with waxed paper and let cool for 45 minutes.

Pour filling into chilled tart shell and refrigerate to thoroughly chill.

Spoon or pipe whipped cream onto top of tart and arrange berries on top. Garnish with mint sprigs if desired.

Makes 12 servings

KIM'S YUMMY RHUBARB COBBLER

1 cup flour
3/4 cup rolled oats
1 tsp. cinnamon
1 cup light brown sugar, packed
1/2 cup unsalted butter, melted
1 cup granulated sugar
1 cup water
3 tbsp. cornstarch
1 tsp. vanilla extract
4 cups sliced rhubarb

Our daughter Kim is an inventive maker of desserts, and among them is this to-die-for rhubarb cobbler. The Craigs and the Jacksons cheer when the rhubarb comes in.

—Shirley

Combine first 5 ingredients and press half of the mixture into the bottom of an 8x8″ baking pan.

In large saucepan, cook sugar, cornstarch, water, and vanilla until mixture becomes quite thick. Add sliced rhubarb and mix thoroughly.

Spread rhubarb mix in prepared pan and top with remaining oat mixture. Bake at 350° for 1 hour. Serve with vanilla ice cream or whipped cream.

Serves 8

CAFÉ MOCHA CHEESECAKE

Crust:
1³/₄ cup chocolate wafers, finely crushed (about 30 wafers)
¹/₃ cup butter, melted

Chocolate mix:
2 tbsp. water
2 oz. semisweet chocolate, chopped
2 tbsp. instant espresso granules
2 tbsp. coffee liqueur

Cheese mix:
3 (8-oz.) pkgs. cream cheese, softened
2 tbsp. flour
1 tsp. vanilla extract
1 cup sugar
4 eggs

Chocolate and coffee make this cheesecake a winner. The recipe looks longer than it actually is.

—Shirley

In bowl, combine crushed wafers and melted butter. Press mixture firmly into the bottom of an 8˝ springform pan. Bake in preheated 375° oven for 8 minutes. Cool and refrigerate.

In small saucepan, combine water, chocolate, and instant espresso granules. Cook over low heat, stirring until chocolate begins to melt. Remove from heat, stir until smooth, then stir in liqueur. Let cool.

In large mixing bowl, beat together cream cheese, flour, vanilla, and sugar until smooth. Add eggs all at once, beating on low speed just until mixed. Do not over-beat. Reserve 2 cups of the cheese mixture, cover, and chill.

Stir cooled chocolate mixture into remaining cheese batter until well blended. Pour this chocolate mixture into chilled crust. Place springform pan on baking sheet and bake in pre-heated 350° oven for 20–25 minutes or until sides are set. Center will be a bit soft. Remove reserved cream-cheese mixture from refrigerator 10 minutes before needed to soften.

With cake still in oven, slide springform pan forward enough to pour reserved cream-cheese mixture over the top of the cake and spread evenly over surface. Bake cake for another 20–25 minutes, until center is set when lightly shaken. Remove from oven and cool completely, then chill for 24 hours before serving.

Optional garnish: Decorate top of cake with chocolate, drizzled in a grid pattern, before serving. YUM!

"By my faith, yes!
Tarte a la crème! . . .
How indebted I am to you,
Madame,
to have reminded me of
tarte a la crème!"
—Molière, *La Critique de l'Ecole des femmes*

TONI'S EVIL LEMON SPONGE PUDDING CAKE

1/4 cup unsalted butter
3/4 cup plus 2 tbsp. sugar
4 eggs, separated
1/4 cup flour
3/4 cup milk
1/2 cup fresh lemon juice
Grated rind of 1 lemon
Pinch salt
Confectioners' sugar

Shirley's friend Toni Chute served this cake to Shirl, who, when she had taken one bite, threatened Toni with immediate harm if she didn't give Shirl the recipe too.

Unintimidated, Toni gave her the recipe anyway.

—Phil

Cream together butter and 3/4 cup sugar. Add the egg yolks, 1 at a time, beating well after each addition. Blend in the flour, milk, lemon juice, and rind.

In another mixing bowl, beat the egg whites with a pinch of salt and the remaining 2 tbsp. of sugar. When whites form soft peaks, stir one quarter of them into the batter. Fold in remaining beaten whites.

Spoon batter into a buttered 1 1/2 qt. baking dish. Place baking dish in a large roasting pan. Pour hot tap water around dish to halfway up sides. Transfer roasting pan to oven and bake pudding for 45–50 minutes or until pick (inserted into the top only) comes out clean.

Indulge!

LEMONY RUM CAKE

Cake:

1 cup chopped pecans

1 (18 1/2 oz.) lemon cake mix

1 (3 3/4 oz.) Jell-O instant lemon flavored pudding mix*

4 eggs

1/2 cup cold water

1/2 cup vegetable oil

1/2 cup dark rum

*If using cake mix with pudding already in the mix, omit pudding, use only 3 eggs, and diminish amount of oil to 1/3 cup.

Glaze:

1/4 lb. butter

1/4 cup water

1 cup granulated sugar

1/2 cup dark rum

Melt butter for glaze. Stir in water and sugar. Boil 5 minutes, stirring constantly. Remove from heat and stir in rum.

Preheat oven to 350°. Grease and flour a 10″ tube pan or a 12-cup Bundt pan. Sprinkle nuts over bottom of pan.

Mix all cake ingredients together (as directed on box), adding rum at the end, and pour batter over nuts. Bake 1 hour (50–55 minutes for Bundt pan).

Invert on serving plate. Prick top and sides. Brush, or pour, warm glaze over entire cake, repeating until all glaze is absorbed.

Note: You may want to halve the glaze recipe. It makes quite a lot.

Lemon and rum: how can you go wrong with a cake that uses lemon, rum, and pecans? This one oozes good flavors. The Craigs and Jacksons like it warm, just out of the oven.

—Shirley

BETE NOIRE (A Chocoholic's Dream)

8 oz. unsweetened chocolate
4 oz. semi- or bittersweet chocolate
$^1/_2$ cup water
$1^1/_3$ cups sugar
$^1/_2$ lb. unsalted butter, room temperature and cut into small pieces
5 extra large eggs at room temperature

Preheat oven to 350°.

Chop both chocolates into fine pieces and set aside.

There are four basic food groups: chocolate, chocolate, chocolate, and chocolate.

—Anon.

Combine water with 1 cup of the sugar in heavy $1^1/_2$ qt. saucepan. Bring to rapid boil over high heat, and cook for about 2 minutes. Remove pan from heat and immediately add chocolate pieces, stirring until completely melted. Add butter, piece by piece, stirring to melt completely.

Place eggs and remaining $^1/_3$ cup sugar in bowl. For a crunchy crust on cake: beat eggs and sugar with electric mixer until they have tripled in volume. For a smoother top: mix eggs and sugar only until sugar is dissolved.

Add the chocolate mixture to the eggs and mix until blended. Do not over-beat.

Spoon mixture into a 9″ cake pan that has been buttered and had bottom lined with buttered parchment paper. Set pan into a slightly larger jelly-roll pan and place on center oven rack. Pour hot water into larger pan. Bake in preheated oven for 25–30 minutes. Let cool in pan for 10 minutes. Run knife around sides of pan to release cake. Cover with plastic wrap and unmold onto cookie sheet.

Invert serving plate over cake and flip it over so cake is on plate. Serve warm with whipped cream or with a Chocolate Ganache (recipe follows).

Serves 8–10 lucky chocolate lovers

CHOCOLATE GANACHE

1 cup heavy cream
10 oz. bittersweet chocolate, cut into small pieces

Scald the cream and remove from heat. Immediately add chocolate and stir gently until smooth. Cool slightly and pour over cake.

A small amount of liqueur may be used to flavor ganache if desired.

The only two ingredients give you a clue: heavy cream and chocolate! Oh, my!

—Zee

REALLY GOOD CARROT CAKE

2 cups flour
2 tsp. cinnamon
2 tsp. baking soda
2 tsp. double-acting baking powder
1 tsp. salt
2 cups peeled and grated carrots
2 cups sugar
1 cup canola oil
4 large eggs, unbeaten
1 cup chopped pecans

There are carrot cakes, and there are carrot cakes. This recipe makes one of the very best. Zee and J.W. grow their own carrots and eat them in many dishes.

—Phil

Mix all dry ingredients, except sugar, together. In separate bowl, beat sugar and oil together with electric mixer. Add dry ingredients, alternately with eggs, to the sugar and oil, mixing well after each addition. Fold in carrots and nuts.

Pour batter into greased and floured 9″ tube pan. Bake in preheated 350° oven for 1 hour. When cool, frost with Cream Cheese Frosting (recipe follows).

CREAM CHEESE FROSTING

¹/₄ lb. unsalted butter (softened)
8 oz. cream cheese (softened)
1 lb. box (approximately) confectioners' sugar
2 tsp. vanilla extract

Beat butter and cheese together until well blended. Blend in sugar and vanilla (using just enough sugar to make desired spreading consistency). Spread over cooled carrot cake.

Note: Makes about 4 cups of frosting. You may want to halve the recipe.

PEACH ROYALE

4 ripe peaches, peeled and sliced
¹/₄ cup Grand Marnier (or other orange-flavored liqueur)
1–2 tbsp. granulated sugar
1 pint vanilla or peach ice cream

Sprinkle half of the sliced peaches with the sugar.

Pour the liqueur over all and marinate in the refrigerator all day, stirring occasionally. Divide marinated slices between four serving dishes and top each with a scoop of ice cream. Place additional peach slices on top and drizzle with more liqueur.

Serves 4–6

Simple, delicious, and elegant, this dish offers a rich and satisfying conclusion to a good dinner. You do most of the work hours before you serve.

—Phil

FLAN

¹/₃ cup sugar
6 eggs
6 tbsp. sugar
2 cups milk
1 tsp. vanilla

*A traditional Spanish
and Mexican dessert.
J.W. makes flan using
a recipe he got from a
Spanish cookbook he
found in a yard sale.
This recipe may be
found in the back of*
Vineyard Enigma.

—Shirley

Set a baking pan, large enough to contain a 9″ pie pan, in a 350° oven and fill with enough water to come up the side of pie pan when filled.

In small frying pan over medium heat, melt the ¹/₃ cup sugar. Shake and tilt pan rather than stirring sugar. Once melted, sugar will caramelize quickly. Wearing hot mitts, since metal pan will get very hot, pour immediately into 9″ pie pan and tilt pan to coat bottom (and part of sides) evenly with syrup. If syrup hardens too quickly, set pan on medium heat until it softens again.

Beat eggs together with 6 tbsp. sugar, milk, and vanilla. Set caramel-lined pan in hot water in oven and pour in egg mixture. Bake at 350° for about 25 minutes. Test doneness by pushing custard in center with back of a spoon. When done, a crevice about ³/₈″ deep forms.

Remove from hot water and chill at once. When cold, loosen flan edge with a knife and cover with a rimmed serving dish. Holding dish in place, quickly invert. To serve, cut in wedges and spoon any remaining syrup over each serving.

Serves 6

MOCHA FLAN

3 tbsp. sugar
3 eggs
¹/₄ cup sugar
¹/₄ tsp. salt
1 tsp. vanilla extract
3 cups scalded milk
2 tsp. instant coffee granules
1 tbsp. rum or brandy

Put sugar in small iron skillet or heavy-bottomed saucepan and place over low heat. Cook until foamy and golden. Immediately pour into 6 custard cups and coat bottoms evenly by tilting cups. Preheat oven to 350°.

Beat eggs lightly to blend. Beat in sugar, salt, and vanilla. Heat milk to scalding (when small bubbles begin to appear around outside edge). Stir in instant coffee and mix until dissolved. Pour slowly over egg mixture, beating with a whisk to keep smooth. Add the rum or brandy.

Pour into custard cups and place in a shallow baking pan lined with paper toweling. Pour 1″ of hot (not boiling) water into the baking pan, and bake for about 45 minutes. Do not let water come to a boil.

The flan is done when a slim knife inserted into center comes out clean.

Chill until cool. Unmold on to individual dessert plates.

Serves 6

This is another nice dessert following a Mexican or Spanish meal. The secret ingredients are coffee granules and rum or brandy.

—Shirley

FRUIT IN MASCARPONE CUSTARD

6 medium ripe peaches or pears
1 tsp. sugar
4 tbsp. butter
$^1/_2$ cup sugar
1 egg
$^2/_3$ cup Mascarpone cheese
2 tbsp. flour

*As you might guess, the
key ingredient here is
Mascarpone, a sinfully
rich cheese that costs an
arm and a leg. There are
substitutes for
Mascarpone and some
of them are good, but
none of them are as
good as Mascarpone.
Once you have the
cheese, the rest of the
recipe is easy and, of
course, delicious.*

—Phil

Peel, core, and slice fruit. Arrange slices in buttered baking dish. Sprinkle 1 tsp. sugar over top.

Cream butter and the $^1/_2$ cup of sugar together until light and fluffy. Beat in egg, then the Mascarpone. Stir in flour and mix well. Spoon mixture over fruit and bake in pre-heated 350° oven just until set (about 20 minutes).

Serves 6

GRAPES WITH SOUR CREAM AND BROWN SUGAR

¹/₄–¹/₂ tsp. grated orange rind
²/₃ cup dairy sour cream
2 tbsp. light brown sugar
¹/₂ tsp. vanilla extract
2¹/₂–4 cups seedless green grapes

Mix sour cream, sugar, vanilla, and orange rind together.
Beat until sugar is completely dissolved. Add washed and
dried grapes to mixture and toss lightly. If grapes are sour,
add a little more vanilla and sugar.

Cover mixing bowl with plastic wrap, and refrigerate until
serving time. Serve in pretty serving bowl or in individual
serving dishes, garnished with mint sprigs.

Serves 6–8

*This amazingly simple
dish is also amazingly
good and amazingly
popular. It's a fine, light
dessert that almost
everyone enjoys.*

—Shirley

PEACH MELBA

1 can (29-oz.) cling peach halves in heavy syrup
1 vanilla bean
1 pkg. (10-oz.) frozen raspberries thawed (or French
raspberry preserves)
$\frac{1}{2}$ cup sugar
1 tbsp. cherry liqueur
Vanilla ice cream

Nellie Melba also got a piece of toast named after her, which may suggest that one could nibble on Nellie from morning until night, from breakfast until after dinner. She must have been a tasty morsel.

—J.W.

Drain peaches; reserve syrup. Pour syrup into 3-qt. saucepan; add vanilla bean. Heat to boiling: boil uncovered over medium heat for 2 minutes. Remove from heat; add 6 peach halves. Refrigerate, covered, until cold (at least 3 hours).

Drain raspberries (if using frozen berries); reserve $\frac{1}{2}$ cup syrup. Place raspberries in blender and blend on high speed until pureed; reserve. Pour raspberry syrup into 2-qt. saucepan and add sugar. Heat to boiling; boil, uncovered, over medium heat, 8 minutes. Add raspberries: boil 1 minute. Remove from heat; stir in cherry liqueur. Refrigerate, covered, until cold (may be prepared to this point, 24 hours in advance). If using French raspberry preserves as topping, omit sugar and procedure for processing frozen raspberries.

At serving time, drain peach halves. Place thick slice of ice cream in bottom of each of six individual dessert dishes. Place 1 peach half, cut side down, on each serving. Spoon raspberry sauce or preserves over peaches; serve immediately.

Serves 6

LACE COOKIE CYLINDERS

1½ cups rolled oats
1½ cups light brown sugar
2 tbsp. flour
½ tsp. salt
⅔ cup melted, unsalted butter
1 egg, slightly beaten
½ tsp. vanilla extract

Mix first 4 ingredients together. Stir in melted butter, then add egg and vanilla and combine well. Drop the batter by teaspoons full, 6 at a time, about 2 inches apart on ungreased baking sheet. Bake in preheated 350° oven for 8–10 minutes (just until lightly browned). Remove from oven and let cookies stand on sheet for 1 minute or just until firm enough to turn with spatula. Turn cookies over on sheet and, working quickly, roll them into cylinders. If cookies become too hard to roll, return to oven for a few seconds to soften. Repeat with remaining cookie dough.

Makes about 30 cookies

These cookies are fun to make, interesting in appearance, and addictive. Get a fellow cook to join you in the kitchen and help roll them out, while you catch up on the local gossip.

—Shirley

MOLASSES SUGAR COOKIES

³/₄ cup soft shortening (butter flavored is good)
1 cup sugar
¹/₄ cup New Orleans–style molasses
1 egg
2 cups flour
2 tsp. baking soda
1 tsp. ground cinnamon
¹/₂ tsp. ground cloves
¹/₂ tsp. ground ginger
¹/₂ tsp. salt

This classic recipe is a favorite with J.W. and Zee and their kids, Joshua and Diana. Every cook should have a recipe for Molasses Sugar Cookies.

—Shirley

Cream together shortening and sugar until light and fluffy. Add molasses and egg and beat well.

Mix remaining dry ingredients together well and add to first mixture, mixing well.

Cover and chill dough for at least ¹/₂ hour (1 hour is better).

Form dough into 1″ balls and roll in granulated sugar. Place on cookie sheet (Zee likes the insulated ones) 2″ apart. You may flatten the balls slightly with a decorative cookie stamp or the bottom of a glass.

Bake in preheated 375° oven for 8–10 minutes. Cool on wire racks.

Makes about 4 dozen cookies

COFFEE-SPICE COOKIES

1 cup soft shortening (butter flavored is good)
2 cups light brown sugar (or brownulated sugar)
2 eggs
$\frac{1}{2}$ cup cold coffee
3$\frac{1}{2}$ cups flour
1 tsp. baking soda
1 tsp. salt
1 tsp. ground nutmeg
1 tsp. ground cinnamon

Cream shortening and sugar together until light and fluffy.
Beat in eggs. Stir in cold coffee.

Mix dry ingredients together well and stir into first mixture.

Chill dough, covered, for an hour.

Another favorite with
the Jackson kids.

—Zee

Form into 1″ balls or drop by rounded teaspoons, 2″ apart,
on lightly greased baking sheet.

Bake in preheated 400° oven for about 8–10 minutes or
until almost no imprint remains when touched lightly with
finger. Cool on wire racks.

Makes about 5 dozen cookies

NANA'S STEAMED PUDDING

Sift together:

2 cups unbleached flour

1 tsp. baking soda

1 tsp. salt

1 tsp. cinnamon

$^1/_2$ tsp. powdered cloves

Mix together:

1 cup light New Orleans molasses

$^3/_4$ cup melted margarine

$^1/_2$ cup warm milk

2 beaten eggs

Welcome to the winter solstice! This dessert is traditional for winter festivities. I learned how to make it from my Prince Edward Island grandmother. The recipe may be found at the back of First Light.

—Shirley

Add dry ingredients to wet ingredients in stages. Add:

1 pint jar of mixed candied fruits

1 cup of seedless raisins that have been plumped in hot water and well dried

Dredge fruits in flour, shaking off excess, before adding to batter.

Stir in 2–3 oz. of good brandy (everyone in the family should give a stir to ensure that they will be together until the next holiday season).

Pour batter into well-greased and floured steamer mold. Place steamer in a large pot of boiling water with a rack at the bottom (water should reach about two-thirds of the way up the sides of the mold), cover pot, and steam (water should simmer continuously) for 2 hours. Cool on wire rack before unmolding.

Serve with hard sauce or lemon sauce. (Recipes follow.)

HARD SAUCE

¹/₄ lb. soft unsalted butter
1 cup granulated sugar (some prefer confectioner's sugar)
1 tsp. vanilla extract
1 oz. each of rum and brandy

Cream butter and sugar until light and fluffy. Add remaining ingredients and beat well. Mound in a pretty bowl. Sprinkle with nutmeg before serving, and top with maraschino cherry. Serve over warm steamed pudding.

LEMON SAUCE

¹/₄–¹/₂ cup sugar
1 tbsp. cornstarch
1 cup water

Combine above ingredients in top section of double boiler which is over, but not in, boiling water. Stir until thickened. Remove from heat and stir in:

2–3 tbsp. butter
¹/₂ tsp. grated lemon rind
1¹/₂ tbsp. lemon juice
¹/₈ tsp. salt

Serve warm over steamed pudding.

BAKLAVA (Nut and Phyllo Pastry)

1¹/₂ lbs. phyllo
1 lb. ground walnuts (can be done in food processor)
¹/₂ tsp. cinnamon
¹/₄ cup sugar
1 lb. unsalted butter, melted

Syrup:
4 cups sugar
2 cups water
1 tbsp. lemon juice
¹/₄ cup honey

This classic Greek dessert is so sweet that it can almost make your teeth hurt. Buttering the phyllo takes a little time, but the result is worth it. You can eat your baklava right away, enjoy it over several days, or freeze it, because it is very, very rich. Baklava makes you wish you were Greek, if you're not already.

—J.W.

Stir sugar and water together (for syrup) in a small saucepan until sugar is dissolved. Bring to a boil, add honey and lemon juice, and simmer for 15 minutes. Set aside to cool.

Mix ground nuts, sugar, and cinnamon together.

Line a buttered 9x13″ baking pan with 10 pieces of phyllo, brushing each layer with melted butter. Spread a thin layer of nut mixture over top layer.

Butter 3 more layers of phyllo and again spread a thin layer of nut mixture on top layer. Continue in this manner until all of the nut mixture is used up.

Top with 10 more layers of phyllo, brushing each layer with melted butter. Put aside until butter sets. Cut into 1¹/₂″ diamonds before baking.

Bake in preheated 375° oven for about 40 minutes or until golden and crisp. Pour cooled syrup over hot baklava.

Makes about 50 pieces

ZEPPOLIS

3 eggs
1 lb. Ricotta cheese
2 tbsp. sugar
4 (yes, 4!) tbsp. baking powder
3 tbsp. brandy or cognac (or liqueur of your choice)
2 tbsp. lemon zest
Wondra Flour (only if necessary)

Mix all ingredients, except flour, together and chill for at least 1 hour. Fry large spoonfuls in 375° vegetable oil until golden. If batter doesn't hold together when frying, add a little Wondra Flour. Turn to fry both sides. Remove from oil with slotted spoon and drain well on paper towels. Keep warm in oven until all batter is fried. While still hot, sprinkle with confectioners' sugar and serve with your choice of coffee.

Serves 4–6

Another goodie from the Mediterranean. They know how to cook over there!

—J.W.

LIGHT FRUIT CAKE

1 lb. (4 cups) pecan halves
1/2 lb. (2 cups) California walnut halves
3/4 lb. (2 cups) whole candied cherries
1/2 lb. (2 cups) diced candied pineapple
1 1/2 cups light raisins
1 cup sifted all-purpose flour
***
1 1/2 cups butter or margarine
1 1/2 cups sugar
3 eggs
1 oz. (or 2 tbsp.) lemon extract
2 cups sifted all-purpose flour
3/4 tsp. baking powder
Light corn syrup
Red and green candied cherries

This is the best fruit cake J.W. has ever eaten! It costs a lot of money to buy the ingredients, but is worth every cent. Basically, it's nuts and candied fruits held together with a minimum of dough. Even if you don't like fruit cake, you'll like this one; if you don't, it means you're dead but just don't know it.

—Phil

In large mixing bowl, combine pecans, walnuts, the 3/4 lbs cherries, the pineapple, and the raisins. Toss with the 1 cup of flour; set aside.

Cream together butter or margarine and sugar 'til light and fluffy. Add eggs 1 at a time, beating well after each addition. Stir in lemon extract.

Sift together the 2 cups flour and the baking powder and add, in thirds, to the creamed mixture; mix well.

Add batter to fruit, mixing well to coat all fruits and nuts. Transfer batter to a well-greased 10″ tube pan. Cover tightly with foil.

Place a pan of hot water on the bottom oven rack. Bake cake on shelf above the water in 300° oven for 2¹/₂ hours. Remove foil; bake 3–5 minutes or 'til top is slightly dry.

Remove cake from pan when cooled thoroughly. Store in tightly covered container. Before serving, brush with light corn syrup, garnish with poinsettias cut from candied cherries.

Drinks

"THE MANY NEW BREWPUBS THAT ARE
SPRINGING UP ALL OVER THE COUNTRY
. . . OFFER THE BEST EVIDENCE WE
HAVE THAT THE NATION IS NOT,
AFTER ALL, GOING TO THE
DOGS, BUT IS ACTUALLY
IMPROVING. ALL THAT
MICROBREWERY BEER
SUGGESTS A FUTURE
FULL OF HOPE."

—J.W., IN *VINEYARD SHADOWS*

SUN TEA (A No-Brainer)

Sun tea is simple to make and for some reason tastes better than tea made from hot water. It is a perfect thirst quencher on a hot summer day. Put some ice cubes in a tall glass, fill the glass with sun tea, and drink deep. Ahhh!

—Phil

1 gal. cold water
7 tea bags (or amount to make the strength you like)

Put both ingredients in a 1-gal. glass jug, with lid. Cover and set in a sunny spot for several hours. Remove tea bags, when brew looks strong enough, and refrigerate. Serve in tall glasses over ice. Offer with lemon slices and sugar for those who don't take their tea neat.

This brewing method produces a clear, smooth iced tea.

THE PERFECT MARTINI

There are books containing long and learned arguments about what constitutes "the perfect martini." James Bond likes his shaken, not stirred. J.W. drinks vodka martinis, using the best vodka he can afford that day. Here is a good recipe.

—Shirley

Always keep your vodka in the freezer.

Chill a martini glass. Swish a bit of dry vermouth* around the interior and toss it out. Add 2 olives (Zee likes black ones) and Luksusowa vodka straight from the freezer. Voila!

*J.W. actually doesn't use vermouth because back in the late 1940s or early 1950s, when the United States was experimenting with atomic bombs out in Nevada, a scientist attached a bottle of Noilly Prat Dry Vermouth to the bottom of a bomb that was to be detonated. When the explosion occurred, the bottle and its contents were vaporized, and J.W. believes that ever since then you can get just the right amount of vermouth from fallout.

RUM PUNCH

In a tall glass or 16-oz. beer mug place:

1–2 oz. rum (light or dark or both) and several ice cubes

Fill remaining glass half and half with

Cran-Mango juice and Pineapple-orange-banana juice

Drink.

This is also a very good drink without the rum. On warm summer days, J.W. and Zee drink the kind with rum; their children drink the kind without.

—Phil

FIVE-POUND BEER

5 lbs. sugar
5 gals. water
3 pkgs. Fleishman's yeast
$\frac{1}{2}$ can Blue Ribbon Malt Extract

Put ingredients into a clean plastic garbage can, seal lid, attach an air lock (some people use a balloon) to allow gas to escape but to keep air out. When fermentation stops, bottle beer, putting $\frac{1}{2}$ tsp. of sugar into each bottle (to create a secondary fermentation) before capping the bottle. Store in a cool place out of the sun, because heat can cause the bottles to explode.

Five-pound beer was made by home brewers long before modern beer-making kits and supplies were available. It is a golden, bubbly, slightly sweet beer. J.W. has made this beer, but prefers certain commercial brands such as Sam Adams. His tastes run to bitters, amber ales, India Pale Ales, and other British-style beers.

—Zee

SANGRIA

This is a classic Spanish thirst quencher that goes well with or without a summer meal. There is no agreed-upon recipe for the drink, but this one is as good as any Shirl and I have tried. We got the recipe while living in Spain.

—Phil

1 qt. dry red wine (Merlot is good)
$1/2$ cup brandy
$1/4$ cup sugar
3 tsp. fresh lemon juice (or to taste)
1 large orange, sliced
3–4 lemon slices
16 oz. lemon soda—"Limonata" is good (distributed in U.S. by Sanpellegrino)

Mix, adding soda just before serving with ice.

WATER

When we visit Bath, England, a beautiful little city famous for its supposedly healing waters, we always note a statue of a woman pouring from a pitcher. The inscription on the statue reads, "Water is best." Could be.

—Shirley

Open tap, fill glass, add ice. Drink.

Menus

"A VINEYARD MEAL, THE GIFT OF
THE EARTH AND SEA."

-J.W., IN *VINEYARD FEAR*

(ISSUED FIRST AS *CLIFF HANGER*)

Note: The recipes for all starred items are in this book and are listed in the index.

SAILING BRUNCH MENU

J.W. and his family enjoy
lunches like this one
while sailing the Shirley
J. So do Shirl and I.

—Phil

Bloody Marys

Gazpacho*

Eggs Stuffed with Caviar*

Individual Spanakopitas*

Asparagus Roll-Ups*

Dolmas*

Fruit cups with Triple Sec

Lace Cookie Cylinders*

Coffee (with or without Irish Cream)

FULL CREAM TEA

Shirley brought this
menu home from the
Pump Room in Bath,
England. J.W. has never
been to Britain, but he
loves this meal. He
considers it quite posh.

—Phil

English Scones*

Devonshire Cream*

Strawberry jam

Hot tea

BEACH PICNIC

"Wrap" sandwiches

Carrot Penny Salad*

Black Bean and Rice Salad*

Cold Oven-Fried Chicken*

Condiments, such as:

Bread and Butter Pickles*

Crudités to dip in hummus

Apricot Squares*

Or

Molasses Sugar Cookies*

Seasonal fruit

Sun Tea*

There are a lot of picnics on Martha's Vineyard beaches. They offer fare that ranges from simple to regal. This is a good one.

—Zee

This menu can be fancied up with items from the Sailing Brunch Menu and, of course, must include kid favorites for the unadventurous eaters in your party (you know what and who those are). J.W. would, undoubtedly, include some barley pops (beer).

Don't forget to include a large beach blanket, unbreakable eating and drinking utensils, napkins, wet wipes, and extra plastic bags for litter disposal.

ITALIAN MENU

Hors d'oeuvre:

Herbed Eggplant Slices*

Entrée:

Spinach Lasagna*

Salad:

6 fresh tomatoes, sliced and layered with slices of fresh Mozzarella cheese, drizzled with the following dressing.

Dressing:

Who doesn't love Italian food?

—Shirley

2 tbsp. extra virgin olive oil
2 tbsp. balsamic vinegar
$1/4$ tsp. freshly ground black pepper
6 large sweet basil leaves, sliced into thin strips
Mix together and pour over tomatoes and cheese.

Bread:

Wedges of warm Focaccia Bread*

Dessert:

Zeppolis* or Fruit in Mascarpone Custard*

Cappuccino or espresso

This menu will serve 6

GREEK MENU

Hors d'oeuvres:

Taramosalata (Salted Fish Roe Dip)*

Dolmas (Stuffed Grape Leaves)*

Tzatziki (Cucumber/Yogurt Dip)*

First course:

Avgolemono (Egg/Lemon Soup)*

Entrée:

Moussaka (Baked Eggplant with Meat and Béchamel Sauce)*

Aligot (Potato Puree)*

Greek Salad*

Pita bread

Dessert:

Baklava (Nut and Phyllo Pastry)*

Ouzo, if you're feeling adventurous

We loved Greece from the moment our feet touched the ground and felt history oozing up from the ancient earth of Athens. We loved it even more when we tasted Greek food and drink and gazed out upon the wine-dark sea.

—Phil

Turn on some balalaika music and toast Shirley Valentine or Zorba!

SPANISH MENU

Tapas (Spanish appetizers)

Calamari (Fried Squid Rings)*

Mushrooms in Garlic Sauce*

A variety of olive and toasted nuts

Sangria*

Soup:

Gazpacho*

Entrée:

Paella a la Valenciana*

Orange/Onion/Avocado Salad*

Crusty garlic bread or rolls

Dessert:

Mocha Flan*

We lived in a white house in a small town on the coast south of Barcelona. It was off-season and the tourists were all gone. We sat in Maricel's café at lunchtime and drank cold beer and wine and ate Calamari a la Romana, and life was good.

—Shirley

THANKSGIVING MENU

Smoked or Grilled Turkey*

Herb and mushroom stuffing (packaged herbed stuffing mix to which you've added sautéed mushrooms)

Make-Ahead or Madeira Gravy*

Sweet Potato Casserole*

Garlic Mashed Potatoes*

Green Beans with Shallot Butter*

Corn Casserole with Jalapeño Peppers and Cheese*

Julienne Beets and Carrots*

Cranberry/Orange Relish with Ginger*

Cornbread* or purchased rolls

Pecan Pie*

Pumpkin Pie*

The great American harvest festival features tables bending under meats, root vegetables, and, especially, turkey and all the fixings. Here is one of our typical menus.

—Shirley

CLAMBAKE DELUXE

Cold beer and soft drinks

Littlenecks on the Half-Shell*

Clams Casino*

Stuffed Quahogs*

New England Clam Chowder*

Steamed Clams*

Watermelon

Clambakes come in many sizes and shapes. This menu includes the classic ingredients.

—Phil

*See At-Home Clambake (page 100) for additional ingredients and preparation.

A NOTE OF THANKS

Thanks are owed to several people who knowingly or unknowingly contributed significantly to this book. Two of them, alas, have passed on since we began organizing these recipes. They were Shirl's mother, Gen Prada, who assisted with the compilation of the recipes, and our dear friend Elaine Patt, both of whom were excellent cooks.

Most of the other contributors are friends and relatives whose recipes J.W. and Zee have purloined over the years and have included here. Among these fine cooks are our Vineyard neighbor Neil Patt, our longtime novelist friend and colleague Bill Tapply, Toni Chute, Dr. Thomas Blues, Mimi Adams, Susie Rowland, Joanie Cosselman, Jane Dietterich, our daughter Kimberlie (the chocolate queen of Durango, Colorado), and our granddaughter Jessica.

Thanks, too, to our son Jamie, who kept our computers going during our darkest hours, and to the many people who, at our table, were taste testers of these recipes.

ABOUT THE AUTHORS

Shirley Prada Craig was born and raised on Martha's Vineyard, as were her father and grandfather. After her marriage, she and her husband summered on the Island until, in 1999, they both retired from teaching in America and moved to the Vineyard full-time.

Her baked goods have won many blue ribbons at fairs in both Massachusetts and Colorado, and for several years she sold breads, muffins, vegetables, jams and jellies, a variety of pickles and flowers, and smoked bluefish at the West Tisbury Farmers' Market. She and some of her recipes were featured in *An American Folklife Cookbook* by Joan Nathan.

Philip R. Craig's recipes have appeared in half a dozen cookbooks, including *Words to Eat By, As You Like It*, and *A Taste of Murder*, and he has won blue ribbons for his baked goods in county fairs. He is professor emeritus in English at Wheelock College and is the author of a series of mystery novels set on Martha's Vineyard, featuring ex-cop and amateur cook J. W. Jackson and his wife Zee.

ABOUT THE ILLUSTRATOR

Jack Sherman is an art director and illustrator at *Newsday*. He lives in Northport, New York.

ABOUT THE PUBLISHER

Vineyard Stories is in the business of book development and publishing on the island of Martha's Vineyard, Massachusetts. The focus of this small, independent company is on nonfiction that tells stories of and by islanders. The owners and editors are **Jan Pogue**, a journalist with newspaper experience in Baltimore and Philadelphia, and **John Walter**, a former editor at Washington and Atlanta papers, *USA Today*, and the *Vineyard Gazette*. Ms. Pogue most recently has written commissioned nonfiction for Bookhouse Group, Inc. of Atlanta, and is coauthor of a forthcoming book on the American Cancer Society. Vineyard Stories publications this year include a book on West Tisbury artist Allen Whiting; and, next year, a book on the venerable Edgartown institution, the Charlotte Inn.

ACKNOWLEDGMENTS

The recipe for Lobster, Croissants, and Champagne is reprinted with the permission of Scribner, an imprint of Simon & Schuster Adult Publishing Group, from DEAD IN VINEYARD SAND by Philip R. Craig. Copyright ©2006 by Philip R. Craig.

The recipes for Scallops in Wine, Scallops Tikka, and Scallops in Sherry-Mustard Sauce, and the quotation on page 85 are reprinted with the permission of Scribner, an imprint of Simon & Schuster Adult Publishing Group, from VINEYARD PREY by Philip R. Craig. Copyright ©2005 by Philip R. Craig.

The recipes for Bluefish Seviche, Chicken with Snow Peas, and J.W.'s Spaghetti Sauce, and the quotation on page 47 are reprinted with the permission of Scribner, an imprint of Simon & Schuster Adult Publishing Group, from MURDER AT A VINEYARD MANSION by Philip R. Craig. Copyright ©2004 by Philip R. Craig.

The recipes for Kale Soup, Seafood Casserole, and Tom's Sausage, Beans and Rice, and the quotation on page 63, are reprinted with the permission of Scribner, an imprint of Simon & Schuster Adult Publishing Group, from A VINEYARD KILLING by Philip R. Craig. Copyright ©2003 by Philip R. Craig.

The recipes for Chicken Enchiladas, Paella a la Valenciana, and Flan are reprinted with the permission of Scribner, an imprint of Simon & Schuster Adult Publishing Group, from VINEYARD ENIGMA by Philip R. Craig. Copyright ©2002 by Philip R. Craig.

The recipes for New England Clam Chowder, Quick Coq au Vin, and Grilled Vegetables, and the quotations on pages 1, 167, 211, and 245 are reprinted with the permission of Scribner, an imprint of Simon & Schuster Adult Publishing Group, from VINEYARD SHADOWS by Philip R. Craig. Copyright ©2001 by Philip R. Craig.

The recipes for Cream of Refrigerator Soup, Scandanavian Fishbake, and Stuffed Quahogs, and the quotation on page 273, are reprinted with the permission of Scribner, an imprint of Simon & Schuster Adult Publishing Group, from VINEYARD BLUES by Philip R. Craig. Copyright ©2000 by Philip R. Craig.

INDEX